LARGE
PRINT

JOYCE MEYER

100
ways to
Simplify
your Life

FAITH WORDS

LARGE PRINT

FaithWords
Hachette Book Group
237 Park Avenue
New York, NY 10017

Visit our Web site at www.faithwords.com.

Printed in the United States of America

First Edition: August 2007

10 9 8 7 6 5 4 3 2 1

FaithWords is a division of Hachette Book Group, Inc.
The FaithWords name and logo is a trademark of Hachette Book Group, Inc.

LCCN: 2007930155
ISBN 978-0-446-50939-8
ISBN 0-446-50939-6

The Large Print edition published in accord with the standards of the N.A.V.H.

Contents

Introduction

Everyone has them: those days where nothing seems to get done, except maybe what you've added to your already lengthy to-do list. Are you tired most of the time? Are you spent? Do you find yourself wishing for a better day—a simpler day? Too many things compete for your limited resources of attention, energy, and time. You may be suffocating and not even know it. If you feel like this, you're not alone.

Most people today live complicated lives that leave them frustrated and confused, weary and worn out. But I have good news: your life does not have to be that way. You can choose a life of simplicity, fruitfulness, fulfillment, peace, and joy. I want to warn you, however, unless you are determined not to, you will do what everyone else does. You will get sucked up in the system and spend your life wishing things were different, never realizing you are, in fact, the only one who can change things. Unless we are resolute and remain undaunted in our quest for simplicity, we are destined for complication and frustration.

I recall a time when I was complaining to God

about my schedule being absolutely insane. How could anyone be expected to do all I had in front of me? Then the realization hit me that I was the one who made my schedule and nobody could change it but me. You can spend your lives wishing things were different, but wishing won't change anything. Smart decision making and decisive action is what changes things. If you picked up this book looking for change, are you willing to make a decision and follow it up with action?

I wasted many years *hoping* life would change and things would calm down until I finally realized life itself doesn't change; in fact, it has the potential to get worse. I understood my only real option was to change my approach to life. I had to say no to another day of rushing around and feeling frustrated. I didn't want the doctor giving me another prescription to mask another symptom of the real problem—stress.

In my search for simplicity, I have come to believe life can never be simple unless I learn to approach all things simply. It is my attitude toward each event in life that determines how easy or complex each situation will be. Perhaps life is complicated because people are complicated. Is it possible that life is *not* complicated, but rather, individuals complicate life in the way they approach it?

I discovered it wasn't really life or circumstances or other people as much as it was me that needed to change. My problem wasn't the problem—I was the problem! When you spend your life in frustration trying to change the world and everyone in it, you fail to realize it could be you just need to change your approach to life. It can be very easy for someone to live an entire lifetime and never entertain the notion that the way they do things is the real problem.

Have you ever attempted to have friends over for what you initially intended to be a simple afternoon of food, fellowship, and fun, but somehow, it turned into a complicated nightmare? I remember those days vividly. I'd be at church on Sunday and, without much forethought, invite three couples over for the following Sunday to a barbecue. My initial thought was hot dogs and hamburgers on the grill, baked beans, potato chips, and iced tea. My motive was fellowship and fun, but by the time the guests arrived, I didn't even want them there. Fun was not going to happen, at least not for me. Why? I turned my simple get-together into a nightmare of preparation, expensive food, and fourteen people instead of the original six. My complicated approach to life and my complicated thought process convinced me hot dogs and hamburgers weren't nice enough so I bought steaks we could not afford. My potato chips turned into a huge bowl of homemade potato salad. The simple baked beans became four side dishes I labored over.

Insecure and wanting to impress everyone, I had to spend the week cleaning and getting everything in the house to the point where I thought it would be impressive. Of course, the lawn chairs were old, so I bought new ones. I got angry at Dave because I thought he wasn't helping me enough, and by the time our friends arrived, I resented them, wished they hadn't come, and had a miserable day of pretending to be the happy hostess when in reality I was frustrated and miserable.

I could not figure out why I wasn't able to enjoy much of anything in life until God revealed to me I was killing my joy with complication. For years, I prayed God would change the people and circumstances around me when, in reality, He wanted to change me and my approach to life. He wanted me to simplify so, ultimately, He could be glorified.

Let me share with you 100 ways to approach living that can simplify your life and, in turn, release and increase your joy. I believe they will dramatically improve the quality of your everyday experience if you incorporate them into the way you do things. Jesus said He came so we might have *and* enjoy our life in abundance (see John 10:10). His principles are simple. Faith is simple! Trusting God is simple! A childlike approach to Him is simple! The plan of salvation is simple!

Jesus offers us a "new way of living," and I believe it is a simple, yet powerful way that enables us to enjoy everyday life. Are you ready to simplify your life? Are you ready to say good-bye to the complexities you've allowed to take over? Let's get started.

1

Do One Thing at a Time

"The feeling of being hurried is not usually the result of living a full life and having no time. It is, on the contrary, born of a vague fear that we are wasting our life. When we do not do the one thing we ought to do, we have no time for anything else—we are the busiest people in the world."

—Eric Hoffer

Looking away [from all that will distract] to Jesus, Who is the Leader and the Source of our faith [giving the first incentive for our belief] and is also its Finisher [bringing it to maturity and perfection].

—*Hebrews 12:2*

When we do things without truly focusing our minds on them, we immediately decrease our strength to do the work before us and do it well. By putting our hands to one thing and our mind to another, we divide the muscle behind our abilities and we make the task much more difficult. It's like removing an egg yolk from the egg white—both can be used separately but the result isn't as effective (or tasty) as it would be if we leave the egg whole. However, by directing all of our faculties to the one thing we are doing on a particular day, at that hour, at that moment, we find it much easier to do. The ability to concentrate and stay focused can only come from discipline.

The apostle Paul tells us in Philippians 4:6 to be anxious for nothing. Anxious people are always trying to live ahead of where they currently are. They spend today trying to figure out tomorrow and the result is the loss of simplicity. God expects us to trust Him with tomorrow just as He instructed the Israelites to do when they crossed the barren wilderness, pressing toward the Promised Land.

Practice living one day at a time; give yourself—your thoughts, your conversation, your energies, every part of you—to the day at hand. Develop an ability to give yourself to what you are doing. You will sense an awareness enabling you to enjoy the current activity, instead of going through each day in a blur of activity and confusing thoughts which leave you drained and exhausted.

Do you fear you will not accomplish as much if you try to live this way? It's true you may not do as much, but you will also enjoy what you do *a whole lot more.* One key to simplicity is realizing that quality is far superior to quantity.

2

Be Satisfied with What You Have

"Contentment is not the fulfillment of what you want, but the realization of how much you already have."

—Anonymous

Let your character or moral disposition be free from love of money [including greed, avarice, lust, and craving for earthly possessions] and be satisfied with your present [circumstances and with what you have]; for He [God] Himself has said, I will not in any way fail you.

—*Hebrews 13:5*

The affluence of our Western culture has created an epidemic of coveting what everyone else has. People crave more and more, yet they don't enjoy what they already possess. A simple person is a satisfied person; they don't crave more of anything, but they do thoroughly enjoy what they have. They trust that more will come in due time.

Does "more" have the ability to make us happy as the world wants us to believe? The answer is No! In fact, the more we have, the more work we must do to take care of it. We may think "more" makes life easier, but in reality, it often complicates the day-to-day. The tenth commandment tells us not to covet;

we aren't to want what others have. Paul states in Philippians 4:11 that he learned how to be content no matter what his circumstances were. Even hearing that statement reminds me of simplicity and ministers comfort to me.

There's nothing wrong with having things, but it is wrong to lust after them. When we feel we cannot be happy without something, we are lusting after it. We should develop the habit of asking God for what we want, and believe He will give it to us if, and when, it is right. This simple approach to life sets us free to *enjoy* life. Life is the journey, not the destination. Those who want to enjoy life must learn to enjoy the journey, which is filled with waiting. Eventually, we reach our destination only to begin again on a new journey to another place; therefore, to never enjoy the journey is to never enjoy life. Make a decision to begin thoroughly enjoying what you have. Thank God for it and be content.

Joyce Meyer

3

Keep God First

"Man's life is of God, not of his goods, however abundant they may be."

—HENRY ALFORD

I will bless you [with abundant increase of favors] and make your name famous and distinguished, and you will be a blessing [dispensing good to others].

—*Genesis 12:2*

I have read many books indicating one cannot be prosperous and also simple. This teaching disturbs me because I believe it is God's will for His people to be prosperous in every area of their lives, including finances and material goods. Psalm 35:27 says that God takes pleasure in the prosperity of His people. I find no scripture saying He is pleased when His people do not have their needs met.

It is true that Scripture says it is hard for a rich man to get into heaven (see Matthew 19:23), but it is not impossible. Money can divert our attention away from God and His will, but it doesn't have to. We should not be afraid of abundance; instead, we should learn how to handle it properly. If we maintain a proper attitude toward money and material things, they can be used to bless many people.

In the realm of religion, it often seems easier to tell people to totally abstain from something rather than trying to teach them how to avoid excessiveness. I refuse to do that because God has created and given us all things to enjoy. We can enjoy abundance without it pulling us away from God or causing us to be greedy. We can be prosperous and still keep God first in our lives.

What sense would it make for me to say I refuse to eat because I am afraid I might overeat? Or, I refuse to sleep because I might sleep too much? It would make no sense at all and neither does it make any sense to say I will take a vow of poverty to keep money from being a temptation in my life. Let me say this again: money and possessions are not the problem; it is an unbalanced attitude toward them that can become the problem! I believe God wants us to have whatever we can handle while still giving Him first place in our lives.

Prosperity and abundance only become a problem when we allow them to own us instead of us owning them. We should use our belongings to bless people—be careful of falling into the trap of using people to get more "stuff." Money is only a problem if we hoard it. The Bible never says money is a problem; it does say the love of money is a problem. Learn to be a channel, not a reservoir. Let things flow to you and through you. God told Abram He would bless him and make him a blessing (see Genesis 12:2).

Giving to others is not only a source of joy in their lives, it can be our joy as well. In fact, the more you give, the happier you are. The more you give, the more you *have* to give because God looks for people He can trust with money. He looks for people who can have money and not become greedy and selfish. The main question to ask ourselves regularly is, "What is my attitude toward money and possessions?" Is God or money first in your life?

I find I never own too much of anything if I am truly led by the Spirit of God. He regularly prunes all of my possessions by continually placing people in front of me who need or desire something I have in abundance. The Bible teaches us that if we have two tunics or coats and someone else has none, we should give them one of ours (see Luke 3:11).

In my own personal search for simplicity, I find being a blessing to others is one of the simple things I can do to increase my joy as well as the joy of others. As a matter of fact, I encourage people to aggressively look for ways to give because the Bible says it is more blessed to give than to receive (see Acts 20:35). God is delighted when He finds someone He can generously bless who will keep Him first and use what they have to be a blessing to others.

4

Live to Glorify God

"Most men seem to live to themselves, without much regard to the glory of God, or the good of their fellow-creatures."

—David Brainerd

So then, whether you eat or drink, or whatever you may do, do all for the honor and glory of God.

—1 Corinthians 10:31

It's important to show God glory through your life, not just through your words or spiritual acts. Start seeing ordinary daily routines as something done for God, not something to check off your list so you can search for God amidst things *you* think are holy. All of life is holy if lived unto the Lord. Colossians 3:23 teaches us to work heartily at every task, "as [something done] for the Lord and not for men."

God assigns us the ordinary things of life as well as spiritual things like prayer, Bible study, and good works. He tells us throughout His Word to go to work, pay our bills, take care of our homes and bodies, fellowship with other believers, enjoy our food, rest, and laugh. When we begin seeing each activity as something done unto the Lord and for His glory, life becomes simple. We aren't caught up in trying to do—we're simply being what God made us to be.

Dividing the sacred from the secular causes us to live disjointed lives where we always rush through the things we see as mundane in order to get to the spiritual activities we feel God is pleased with. How can we "pray without ceasing" unless we realize all of a life lifted up to God becomes a prayer, a type of living intercession?

If I want to look good so I can glorify God, then my exercise, the time I spend fixing my hair and dressing in a fashion that's eye pleasing, becomes a holy thing. If my motive is vanity—if the only reason I do it is for myself and what I can get out of it—then my actions are not holy. Holy things are those consecrated to God. If I am consecrated to God, if I have given Him my life, all of my senses and abilities, all of my possessions, then is it not true that all of me and my life are holy? Everything we do is sanctified if it is done unto Him.

Did you know God actually refers to His children as saints? This does not mean all our behavior can be classified as holy or we never make a mistake, but God sees us through the blood and sacrifice of Jesus. He views us as righteous when we truly place our trust and confidence in His Son (see 2 Corinthians 5:21). When we dedicate our lives to Him and strive daily to please Him in all things, then all things become holy. It is the attitudes of our hearts we discover are most important to God.

What makes life simple is having an intimate relationship with Christ; following His principles, loving Him for who He is and not just for what He can do for us—these things keep life smooth and uncomplicated. Begin to see life as one whole, not something with many divided parts, some of which are suitable for God and others which are not. If any part of my life is not suitable for the Lord, then it is not suitable for me either and should be cut out. Start removing those parts of your life you keep around only for yourself so you will have more room for the parts that glorify and honor God. Let them grow and flourish and watch how easy it becomes.

5 Don't Worry about Tomorrow

"Any concern too small to be turned into a prayer is too small to be made into a burden."

— CORRIE TEN BOOM

So do not worry or be anxious about tomorrow, for tomorrow will have worries and anxieties of its own. Sufficient for each day is its own trouble.

—Matthew 6:34

God gave the Israelites their manna one day at a time. They were not allowed to store any of it up for another time—by doing this, they showed their trust and confidence in God and His promise to provide for them each day. Any time they did collect more than enough for one day, it became rotten and smelled bad. Many people say they have a "stinking, rotten life." They don't mean they smell—I think they're saying they have taken on too much—too much work, too much responsibility, too much to think through and it's *so* much, they have nowhere to put it and much is wasted. They are complicating today trying to gather provision for tomorrow.

In Matthew 6:25–31, Jesus teaches us not to worry about tomorrow but encourages us to believe that if God takes care of the birds and the flowers, surely,

He will take care of us. Each day contains all we can handle—we don't need to be concerned about more than today. It is the gift of grace, God's enabling power and ability of which He gives us just enough to successfully handle whatever comes our way each day. But He won't give us tomorrow's grace today.

When we think about the future with all of its unanswered questions and threatening circumstances, we can feel quite overwhelmed. Our heavenly Father does not give us an extra supply of grace to think on tomorrow's problems and still maintain our peace of mind and joy. To do so would encourage us to worry, to be anxious and to care about concerns that aren't necessarily ready for our attention. God tells us what to do with our cares: cast them on Him and He will take care of us.

Trying to live tomorrow today complicates life. When the disciples asked Jesus to teach them how to pray, one of the things He told them was to ask Father God for their *daily* bread. He was talking about more than the type of bread one might eat at a meal; He was speaking of whatever it would take to supply their needs for human life. Make life simple and take it one day at a time. Don't fear the future, because what you need to deal with tomorrow can only come with tomorrow. It's impossible to deal with tomorrow's problems today. Put your trust in God and allow yourself to enjoy the simple life.

6

Let Go of What Lies Behind

"You build on failure. You use it as a stepping stone. Close the door on the past. You don't try to forget the mistakes, but you don't dwell on it. You don't let it have any of your energy, or any of your time, or any of your space."

—Johnny Cash

Do not [earnestly] remember the former things: neither consider the things of old.

—Isaiah 43:18

In Philippians 3:13, the apostle Paul says one thing he really made an effort in doing was "forgetting what lies behind"—letting go of what already has passed. I believe Paul tried fixing earlier mistakes and discovered how complicated and impossible it was to try and do that. There is only one thing we can do with the past—give it to God! When we let Him take our messes and turn them into miracles, God has the ability to use our mistakes for our great good if we trust Him to do so.

Isaiah 61:3 says He will give us "beauty instead of ashes," but I find a lot of people want to keep their ashes, the cinders of the past, as reminders of their shortcomings and failures. Decide to give up your ashes, or that is all you will ever have. Every day is a new day containing tremendous possibilities: new life, new hopes, and new dreams. We cannot, however, even *see* the possibilities of today if we stay entrenched in the mistakes and disappointments of yesterday. Let go of what's behind and move forward.

It's imperative to get our minds out of the past in order to see God's good plan for today. Abraham was a man who lost plenty. He gave his nephew Lot the best part of the Jordan valley in order to prevent strife, leaving him much less than he owned previously. He could have become filled with self-pity and discouragement, but instead, he listened to God, Who told him this:

> *Lift up now your eyes and look from the place where you are, northward and southward and eastward and westward;*
>
> *For all the land which you see I will give to you and to your posterity forever.*
>
> —*Genesis 13:14–15*

Perhaps you need to look up and around instead of back and down. Lift your eyes and see the amazing future which bursts with hope for you in God! Don't spend your life mourning over what you have lost and what is already gone; take an inventory of what you have left and keep going, one foot in front of the other, one step of faith at a time. Remember, God is on your side!

Learn How to Say No

"The art of leadership is saying no, not saying yes. It is very easy to say yes."

—TONY BLAIR

But let your yes be [a simple] yes, and your no be [a simple] no, so that you may not sin and fall under condemnation.

—*James 5:12*

People don't like the word no, do they? They'll grin from ear to ear when you say yes to something, but you won't see many smiles when they hear you say no. It's natural to want to be loved and accepted—we all want that—but that tendency makes it very easy to fall into the trap of being a people pleaser. This greatly complicates life, however, because different people want and expect a variety of things from us as individuals. Ever hear the phrase "You can't please all the people all the time"? People pleasers quickly find, in order to give everyone everything they want and achieve an end result which keeps them happy, somewhere along the way a hefty price is required—we pay, and lose ourselves.

God created each of us in a unique way; we are individuals who have a right to live our own lives. This does not mean we never adapt and adjust ourselves and our desires in order to help or make others happy, but it does mean we cannot continue to please people at the expense of pleasing God. He is not pleased when we miss fulfilling our own destiny because we're living a frustrated life attempting to keep everyone around us satisfied, but ignoring His desires for us.

I have personally struggled greatly with this. As someone who was sexually abused as a child, I grew up often feeling cast off and devalued. I hated the emotional pain of rejection so much, that I desperately wanted acceptance and was willing to pay just about any price to get it. It didn't take me long to discover, though, that saying yes when I really wanted to say no was stealing my life from me. I resented the very people I was trying to keep happy, and I learned in the long run they were not really true friends.

People who are only willing to be happy with you when they can control you *are using you.* Allowing them to do so not only hurts you, but it also ultimately hurts them. Sadly, most people will do whatever we allow them to do; this seems to be the nature of the fleshly carnal man. Godly confrontation and a refusal to be controlled by people is healthy for all involved and eventually builds great relationships that are fair to both parties.

Make a decision to please God above everything else. Put His will before your own and before the will of other people. If you truly feel in your heart God wants you to say yes, then say it and stick to it; but if you feel He's directing you to say no, then say no and stick to that as well. God always supplies the grace and whatever else is needed to enable us to do whatever He asks us to do—giving us the tools to say no with ease and simplicity. Complication and struggle, just by their mere presence in our lives can often indicate we are out of the will of God. If our hearts say no while our mouths say yes out of fear of rejection, we cannot expect God to help us. He is not obligated to finish anything He did not author.

You are not alone as you learn to say no. Ask God for His supernatural strength and wisdom to guide you toward more simple decision making and feel confident you are following His lead.

8

Be Yourself

"To be yourself in a world that is constantly trying
to make you something else is the greatest
accomplishment."

—RALPH WALDO EMERSON

*But let every person carefully scrutinize and examine and test
his own conduct and his own work. He can then have the
personal satisfaction and joy of doing something commendable
[in itself alone] without [resorting to] boastful comparison with
his neighbor.*

—Galatians 6:4

For many years of my life, I tried to be like other
people. I tried to pray like them, act like them, and
even look like them. After many years of misery and
struggle, I finally realized God would never help me
be anyone but me. There was a reason He made me
the way I am and not like someone else. It is very
complicated trying to be someone else, and there is
absolutely nothing programmed into us that gives us
understanding of how to do that. It is much easier,
much simpler to just be ourselves—God shows us
how to do that because it is His will.

You don't have to compare or compete with anyone or anything else, and that, my friends, is true free-

dom. Jesus came to set people free in many ways, and this is one of them. I want to say again, you don't have to compare yourself or anything about you with other people; you don't have to compete to be like them or better than them (see 2 Corinthians 10:12). All God expects is that we try to be the best we can be. I always say, "He wants me to be the best me I can be." Since I have seen that, I have grown by leaps and bounds.

We can look at others as examples and even be provoked by others to work harder in various areas of our behavior. But we should not allow anyone except Jesus to be our standard. The people to whom Paul ministered were told to follow him as he followed Christ. He said he was an example to them, but he never told people they had to specifically be like him.

Learn how you can relax with others and just be yourself. If they reject you, they reject what God created, not what you have created. Of course, we all have areas we can improve, but only God can do the changing and He does it His way and in His timing. Sometimes we feel so bad about *who* we are, we create a fake personality to show the world. This is usually where we have trouble in relationships. But when we enter into the freedom of simply being who God created us to be, the anointing of God is present and gives us favor with people. I learned to stop trying to make people like me and began trusting God to give me "divine connections."

I have to say, I like me for me, and therefore, other people like me—maybe not everyone, but there are plenty who do, and they keep me busy enough. If you will decide to accept and like yourself for who you are and who God has made you, you will find more acceptance and less rejection.

9 Choose Quality over Quantity

"The quality, not the longevity, of one's life is what is important."

—MARTIN LUTHER KING JR.

Learn to sense what is vital and approve and prize what is excellent and of real value [recognizing what is the highest and the best].

—*Philippians 1:10*

There was a time when society was much simpler than it is today. When we take a moment to look back to those days, we see those were also times when people were more concerned with quality than quantity. Having more is not always better—it is very often worse. We tend to buy cheaper clothes so we can have more clothes, then we become frustrated because they shrink or fade or don't last like we thought they would. Having too many clothes can even make getting dressed complicated. As one man said, "I never had any trouble packing for a trip when all I had was one brown suit and one blue one. I simply packed them both and alternated them during the trip. Now that I have a closet full of clothes, packing has become a complicated ordeal and it takes a long time to decide what goes with what."

If we choose to buy quality products such as appliances and furniture, even when it means having fewer things for a period, we actually save time in the maintenance needed. Poor-quality items break down more often and wear out sooner. The more we have to deal with in life, the more complicated life becomes.

Recently, God spoke to my heart, telling me not to do anything I really don't have to do. If someone else can do it—let them! Following this has helped in my quest to simplify my life. Our lives cannot be simplified until we have a smaller amount of things to deal with. I am determined to find ways to deal with less and yet remain fruitful in my life.

We might purchase an automobile for looks, yet get poor quality and spend a great deal of time taking it in for repairs. Or we may waste time running all over town trying to get a cheaper price on an item and actually spend more in time than we would have spent in money. What is your time worth? Mine is worth a lot to me. I am willing to purchase a higher-quality item if it saves me time.

Develop a habit of buying the best quality item you can get for the money you have available. Don't think more is always better—it is a deception. I would rather buy one good-quality item instead of three or four mediocre or inferior ones.

Refuse to Start What You Cannot Finish

"We rate ability in men by what they finish, not by what they attempt."

—ANONYMOUS

For which of you, wishing to build a farm building, does not first sit down and calculate the cost [to see] whether he has sufficient means to finish it?

—*Luke 14:28*

Multiple unfinished projects clutter our minds and lives. They continually scream at us to finish them and they condemn and mock us. The longer it takes to finish the worse we feel about ourselves. No person can attempt to do everything and do any of it well. We do have limitations and we should not be afraid to face them. God is not limited, and truly, each of us who places faith in Him can do whatever He leads us to do; however, God does not lead people to start things and not finish.

God has begun a good work in each of us and will continue working right up until the day of Christ's return, completing and perfecting that good work (see Philippians 1:6). Some projects are short term and others take longer—impatient people usually do not finish the long-term ones. Spiritual maturity, for example, requires patience. We don't change overnight. There are many people who backslide because they cannot obtain a "drive-through breakthrough." They want instant success and there really is no such thing.

I know people who begin every new project with an abundance of emotional energy, but when the newness wears off, either they leave it for someone else to finish or it never gets finished at all. New things are always exciting, but what about after all the goose bumps and applause is gone? Who is still around then? Only those who counted the cost and knew from the beginning there would be many phases to go through other than the exciting ones. Those who quit and walk away are almost always frustrated and full of excuses for why they can't finish something.

Most people in our society today are addicted to taking on more than they can handle. Stress management has become a billion-dollar business, and most of the stress we experience today is caused by trying to do too much. I always have more on my to-do list than I can finish in one day, but I go after it again the next day. Whatever we take on as a responsibility, we should commit to finishing and doing it well and on time.

Simplify your life by beginning only what you know you can finish and finishing what you begin.

Don't allow yourself to get distracted—stay focused and finish. When you complete something, you no longer need it on your mind. You are free to give yourself completely to the next project, to the next goal, the next big idea in your life. You are free to dream and free to create because your mind and your heart are clutter-free. This is simplicity at its best.

11

Don't Make Mountains out of Molehills

"Better never trouble trouble until trouble troubles you.
For you're sure to make your trouble double trouble
when you do."

—DAVID KEPPEL

Peace I leave with you; My [own] peace I now give and
bequeath to you. Not as the world gives do I give to you.
Do not let your hearts be troubled, neither let them be afraid.
[Stop allowing yourselves to be agitated and disturbed; and
do not permit yourselves to be fearful and intimidated and
cowardly and unsettled.]

—John 14:27

There are too many people today who insist on sweating about the small stuff. They let little details get to them and upset them so much that life is always filled with problems and worries. Someone said, "Choose your battles," and that is wise counsel. There are enough major events in most of our lives that we need to deal with—we certainly don't need to make a big deal out of things we could just as easily ignore.

There are multiple opportunities each day to become upset about something, but we have the choice to let them go and remain at peace. Satan sets us up to get us upset! Locate the things upsetting you and get to know yourself—decide to let go of all the little ones that really don't make any difference in the overall scope of life anyway. The Bible says it is the little foxes that spoil the vine (see Song of Solomon 2:15). How many people get divorces over all of the little things they kept recorded in their hearts that eventually became big mountains they could no longer climb over? If we take no account of the evil done to us as 1 Corinthians 13 instructs us to do, we will have much better, much simpler relationships. At one time, I was a very good "accountant"—I kept account of all the things people did to me that hurt or offended me. My life was also a big mess; it was complicated and I was not happy.

Don't be someone who is easily offended. You will be the one who suffers the most if you are. Usually, when someone offends us, it is never their goal to do so. Get into a habit of believing this and you will take an important step toward a simple life. If our minds are cluttered with thoughts of what everyone has done to us, we definitely won't be able to experience or enjoy simplicity. For life to be simple, our thoughts and emotions must be pure. Our hearts must be fully open to forgiving people instead of receiving hurt or offense.

When we spend an excessive amount of time meditating on what people have done to us instead of what they have done for us we lose our joy. We develop a critical, murmuring, defensive attitude that displeases God. We can see much of the complication of life removed when we become willing to quickly and frequently forgive.

Get Your Mind Off Yourself

"A man is called **selfish** not for pursuing his own good,
but for neglecting his neighbor's."

— RICHARD WHATELY

*And Jesus called [to Him] the throng with His disciples and
said to them, If anyone intends to come after Me, let him deny
himself [forget, ignore, disown, and lose sight of himself and
his own interests] and take up his cross.*

— *Mark 8:34*

Someone with a selfish, self-centered lifestyle is usually also very complex and convoluted. God never intended us to look only inward, only trying to take care of ourselves. He wants us to reach out to others and trust Him to take care of us. The Bible says Jesus trusted Himself and everything to His heavenly Father because He knew He would judge fairly (see 1 Peter 2:23), and we should follow His example.

The entire goal of a Christian should be to follow Jesus. After we make this commitment, Jesus said we would need to lose sight of ourselves including all of our own interests (see Mark 8:34). Many times we think if we turn everything over like He asks, we will never enjoy life or have anything we want, but just the opposite is true. When we give our lives away to others, God gives us a life beyond anything we could ever provide for ourselves. I highly recommend you retire from self-care and let God be God in your life and allow Him to care for you.

I am not saying you should not take care of yourself physically, mentally, emotionally, and spiritually, because you should. I am saying to stop worrying about yourself and how you can get all the things you want out of life. Get yourself off your mind because the more you think about yourself, the more miserable you will be.

Everything in our carnal or human nature is for self-preservation, but thank God, when anyone receives Christ as their Savior and Lord, they receive a new nature (see 2 Corinthians 5:17). That new nature gives us the ability to be self*less*—to put others first before ourselves. We must learn a new way of living once we are "in Christ." We enter into relationship with Him through an *act* of faith—the action we take when we ask Him to be Lord of our life, but we then must learn to live with an *attitude* of faith—the mental position we must hold on to that says, *It's no longer about me.* Deposit yourself with God and embark on a life worth living. Worrying about yourself and always trying to make sure you are taken care of is complicated, but trusting that God will care for you as you care for others is simple.

Refuse to be fearful about what will happen to you. God is faithful and He will take care of you if you trust Him.

13

Stop Procrastinating

"Procrastination is opportunity's natural assassin."

—VICTOR KIAM

Again He sets a definite day, [a new] Today, [and gives another opportunity of securing that rest] saying through David after so long a time in the words already quoted, Today, if you would hear His voice and when you hear it, do not harden your hearts.

—*Hebrews 4:7*

Life feels complicated to me when I have on my mind a dozen projects left to finish. These are things I have either committed to do or know I need to do, but I have not taken action to complete. I cannot enter God's rest until I listen to His direction and take action. We should make sure we actually do what God leads us to do, or do what we know in our hearts we should do. Good intentions do not equal obedience, and until we obey, we will not feel satisfied in our souls.

Procrastination is one of the devil's great deceptions. Through it, he convinces us we will do something, we plan to do it, but we often fail to realize we have not done it. Planning is good, but action is better. How many things lurk in your life right now you know you should do, but have not yet done? I'm sure they are a source of aggravation or even torment for you. Every time you go into the closet you have intended to clean for three years, it condemns you. It screams, "You are lazy and undisciplined" and without even being fully aware of it, the closet makes you feel bad about yourself. The best course of action is to decide on a day to clean the closet and, like the shoe commercial says—just do it!

How about those household repairs you need to complete, or that list of phone calls you've put off for weeks, maybe months? Just thinking about what you still have to do can make you feel lazy and disorganized. These feelings may be vague and subtle, but they are always present and can prevent us from truly enjoying life. The simple thing to do is set a day or a time aside and get the job done! One act of discipline and action will protect you from multiplied days of feeling overwhelmed.

If you are facing a lot of unfinished projects or tasks you have put off way too long, don't get stressed out and allow yourself to feel defeated before you ever begin. Take them one at a time, and simply keep at it until you are finished. Look at the finish line—not the work it will take to get there. You will have to discipline yourself and make some sacrifices along the way, but the dividend will be many days of freedom and enjoyment. The Bible says that no discipline for the present brings joy, but rather grief (see Hebrews 12:11). Nevertheless, later on, it "yields a peaceable fruit of righteousness to those who have been trained by it." Wise people care more about later than now. They are investors—they invest what they have in order to have something better in the future.

Simplify your life today by making a decision to be a "now" person who never procrastinates. Let your new philosophy in life be to "never put off until tomorrow what can be accomplished today." Do it now, and experience the peace that comes with the simple act of doing.

14

Clear Out the Clutter

"Eliminate physical clutter. More importantly, eliminate spiritual clutter."

—D. H. MONDFLEUR

For He . . . is not a God of confusion and disorder but of peace and order.

—*1 Corinthians 14:33*

Clutter always makes me feel overwhelmed and I am the type of person who must clear it out before I can ever start to feel better. My husband tends to want to save things just in case he looks back years from now and realizes he needed that one thing; but my philosophy is if I were to need it five years from now, I probably wouldn't remember where it was anyway, so I should just give it to someone who can use it now and get another if and when I ever do need it again.

If you find yourself cluttered up and done in by disorganization, ask yourself why you seem to hang on to everything that comes your way. Do you feel obligated to keep it just because someone gave it to you? Of course, we don't want to hurt people's feelings, but on the other hand, if a gift is given correctly, it comes with no strings attached. If someone truly gives you a gift, it should be yours to do with as you please.

Quite often, people give you things they like that may not suit your taste at all. Although you deeply appreciate the thought behind the gift, you should not feel obligated to use it. God gives us bread to eat and seed to sow (see 2 Corinthians 9:10), which means some of what He gives us was originally intended to be something we could pass on to someone else.

I once gave a friend an expensive bracelet I owned and, after about two years, I noticed it on another friend's arm and realized she had given it away. For a moment, I was tempted to be hurt but quickly remembered my own guideline. I gave it with no strings attached and had no right to dictate its future. Once given to my friend, it was hers to do with as she liked. The fact that she gave it away did not mean she didn't like it or was unappreciative. It may have been a huge sacrifice for her to give it and she probably did so in obedience to something God asked her to do. Believing in and for the best is always the simple way to approach issues.

In order to keep my surroundings clutter free, I regularly pass things on to other people. I have learned to enjoy it and see it as a way I can give. I like nice things, but I don't want so many I can't enjoy them because everything appears untidy and disorderly.

Many times, the clutter in our lives isn't the fault of others—we're the ones to blame! Do you have so many clothes you become confused trying to get dressed? Do you have so many decorative items sitting around you feel like a bull in a china shop when you try to dust your home? Do you have so much of something that you never use it all before the expiration date runs out? Do you find yourself moving lots of things from place to place but you never actually use or even enjoy them? If your answer is yes to any of these questions, then I believe you need to get bold and clean out the clutter. Get yourself a giving box and fill it up with things someone else will really enjoy but you will never miss. This step will simplify your surroundings and, in turn, clean up the clutter in your spirit and give you a more peaceful, simple way of looking at things.

15

Avoid Excess

"Your body is the baggage you must carry through life. The more excess baggage, the shorter the trip."

—Arnold H. Glasgow

Be well balanced (temperate, sober of mind), be vigilant and cautious at all times; for that enemy of yours, the devil, roams around like a lion roaring [in fierce hunger] seeking someone to seize upon and devour.

—*1 Peter 5:8*

Someone once said, "Excess is the devil's playground." Any time we become excessive in anything, we are no longer in balance. According to God's Word, a lack of balance opens the door for the devil. One of the main things the devil wants to do is steal our joy and push us toward excess. Having anything in amounts beyond our capacity for use complicates our life. It's like watching a small child put his hand in a cookie jar and insisting on pulling out many at once. He is unable to physically remove his hand from the jar, so both his hand and the cookies are stuck! Excess gets complicated!

If you want a simple approach to life, balance is required. Excessive talking causes problems. Excessive eating causes problems. Excessive debt causes problems. Excess is just a problem.

The Bible talks about a process called pruning (see Isaiah 18:5). When the gardener finds one of his trees has excessive or diseased branches, he trims them or cuts them off. Some of the excess branches are referred to as "sucker branches." They grow on the lower part of the tree trunk and, although they suck sap from the tree, they never add to the tree's value because these branches cannot bear fruit. The gardener actually has to get rid of them or they will make the entire tree weak and unattractive.

I remember once when Dave had one of our trees pruned. It was cut back so far I was sure he killed it. I was very aggravated and thought the tree looked positively horrible. He told me if I was patient, the next spring it would be prettier than ever. And sure enough, because the tree was pruned and the excess and useless growth removed, it turned out to be the most attractive tree in our yard.

Don't be afraid to cut back on what you don't really need. I believe it opens the door for God to bless you even more. If you have more possessions than you can possibly use, share them with someone who doesn't have enough. By doing this, you will plant seed for a future harvest in your own life.

There are other excesses we experience other than the material ones. If you need to lose some weight, cut back on your portions and you will gradually see a difference. If you frequently have trouble in relationships due to things you say, you may need to talk a little less and listen a whole lot more. Say no to excess and yes to removing the complexity from your life today.

16

Stay Out of Debt

"Debt is the worst poverty."

—Thomas Fuller

The rich rule over the poor, and the borrower is servant to the lender.

—Proverbs 22:7

One of the worst things that can complicate and spiral our lives into a convoluted, torturous chokehold is financial debt. Excessive debt makes life more complex than it needs to be and places great pressure on the borrower. It also puts a tremendous burden on a marriage. In fact, statistics say that burden is so heavy it is the root cause of many divorces.

Our society makes it very easy to get into debt. Merchants tempt you to buy things now and pay for them later by using credit cards—a billion-dollar industry today in America where that same amount is spent to advertise and persuade people to use even more credit. We live in a time when people are impatient and care very little about the future. They live for the moment, but the cold, hard truth is that tomorrow always comes—and tomorrow, we will be forced to deal with the result of what we did today.

There are probably millions of people who have purchased things in the height of emotion and have experienced the painful pressure for months or even years of trying to pay off the debt. They may no longer even *use* the items they purchased and on which they still owe. It is possible they don't even know where their purchases are—maybe in a closet, maybe in the garage or attic. Sometimes, people purchase things and never ever use them. They see a great sale or a "buy two, get one free" promotion, take their newly bought purchases home, put them away for later, and forget they even have them. We seem to be addicted to *stuff* and most of the *stuff* we think we have to have are the very things complicating our lives and stealing the beauty of the simplicity God wants us to enjoy.

By all means, buy what you need and some of what you want, but don't go into debt to do it. Learn to save money for the things you want. The Bible says, "He who gathers little by little will increase [his riches]" (Proverbs 13:11). My husband has a wonderful, simple plan concerning finances: out of everything you get, give some, save some, and spend some within your borders or according to your ability. If you do that, your borders (ability) will increase and you will never have the pressure and complication of debt.

If you are already in debt, then make a commitment to get out. Don't continue doing what you have done in the past and just make the problem worse. You may have to sacrifice for a while to pay your debt off, but it will be worth it to you. A debt hanging over your head is like an iron weight you're forced to carry everywhere you go. Cut the ties and feel the freedom and simplicity that comes with owing nothing.

Let the Main Thing Be the Main Thing

"When you have nothing left but God, then for the first time you become aware that God is enough."

— Maude Royden

Little children, keep yourselves from idols (false gods)—[from anything and everything that would occupy the place in your heart due to God, from any sort of substitute for Him that would take first place in your life]. Amen (so let it be).

— 1 John 5:21

God is a jealous God, and the only place satisfying to Him is the one He rightfully deserves, which is first place in everything. The only way things can go right in our lives is if we strive to keep God in that place of honor, that place of priority. I say we must strive, because if we put no effort into it, then it never happens. Busyness can quickly get our priorities out of line as well as trick us into the deceitfulness of riches.

When it comes to keeping your priorities straight, we see two different responses in the story of Jesus visiting Mary and Martha. Mary seated herself quickly at the Lord's feet to listen to everything He said, but Martha was busy trying to serve the guests and keep the house clean. She got very upset that

Jesus wasn't making Mary help her, but He told her Mary had made the better choice. He even told Martha she was anxious and worried about many things and missing the main point of His visit (see Luke 10:38–42). That day, Martha's life became very frustrating and complicated while Mary's stayed peaceful and serene.

There was another time when Jesus met a rich young ruler who wanted to know what he had to do to experience eternal salvation. When Jesus told him to sell all he had and give it to the poor and follow Him, the young man went away sad because he had so many possessions (see Luke 18:18–23). His possessions deceived him. He did not realize that God was testing him; had he been willing to give them all up in order to have God, then he would eventually have been given more than he had given away. A great many people make that same mistake. They fearfully hang on to what they have and lose what they could have. They accept "stuff" that can never satisfy like Jesus can. They settle for the good instead of soaring for the great. Make a decision to let the main thing be the main thing in your life. Jesus *is* the main thing!

18

Establish Boundaries

"We love to overlook the boundaries which we do not wish to pass."

—SAMUEL JOHNSON

And He made from one [common origin, one source, one blood] all nations of men to settle on the face of the earth, having definitely determined [their] allotted periods of time and the fixed boundaries of their habitation (their settlements, lands, and abodes).

—Acts 17:26

We see from the scripture above that God sets boundaries and we should set them also. When you have no boundaries in your life, you have no protection. Boundaries are like fences; they keep people and things out of your life that are undesirable. They make things definite rather than vague. Many people are afraid to set boundaries because they think they will offend or anger someone. We must remember we are called by God to follow Him and walk in wisdom. We are not called or required to let other people dictate to us what we must do to keep them happy. There is no doubt we want to make people happy. The Bible even says we should make sacrifices to do good and share with others (see Hebrews 13:16), but this is not to be taken out of context or applied in an out-of-balance way.

My youngest daughter is strict about her privacy. It means a lot to her, so she asks people, including me, not to come to her house without calling first. I admit, at first I had to have a small attitude adjustment, but her request was not wrong at all. I needed to respect her boundaries without having a bad attitude.

No one is exactly alike and all of us have different needs. My oldest daughter is just the opposite of the younger one. She says, "Come over anytime and don't bother to call." However, she has other areas in her life where she has tighter boundaries than my youngest daughter. We not only need to have boundaries of our own, but we also need to respect the boundaries of others. That is one way to get them to respect ours. We may not always understand why people are the way they are, but we need to respect their right to be themselves.

Without boundaries, life gets very complicated, becoming a mixed-up brew of no restraints and no guidelines when it comes to how we do life with others. We will often find ourselves feeling taken advantage of or feel we are in a place we don't want to be, doing something we don't want to do. Saying no is placing a boundary.

We even need boundaries for ourselves. For example, setting high standards we endeavor to live by is setting boundaries. We are saying what we will do and what we won't. If we always say yes to ourselves and other people, then we have no boundaries and life will become extremely frustrating and complicated.

If you have no boundaries and have never learned to respect those of other people, you are not only being foolish, but you are missing the simplicity you could be enjoying. Ask yourself what you need in order to be happy and then set your boundaries accordingly. It is not wrong to do so; in fact, it is very wise.

19

Know Yourself

"Know yourself. Don't accept your dog's admiration as conclusive evidence that you are wonderful."

—Ann Landers

Jesus, knowing (fully aware) that the Father had put everything into His hands, and that He had come from God and was [now] returning to God.

—John 13:3

If we continue on from John 13:3, we see Jesus put on a servant's towel and wash His disciples' feet. What an amazing display of humility and greatness. I believe one of the things enabling Jesus to do this was He knew Himself. He knew who He was, where He came from, and where He was going. He also knew why He was sent. He was not insecure at all, but His confidence was in His Father.

Many people do not know who they are, and it causes them to spend their lifetimes trying to do things they have not been called to do, are not equipped to do, and will surely fail to accomplish. We should not only know what we can do, we should also know what we *can't* do. One of the greatest tragedies I have witnessed as an employer is watching people remain in positions that do not challenge them at all, simply due to fear. In the same way, I have been saddened to watch other people remain in positions quite over their heads, while they are unable or unwilling to admit it.

Why do we have such a difficult time saying, "That is not my strength and I don't think I would do a good job at it"? We are insecure! We get too much of our worth and value from what we do when we should get it from who we are in Christ. If you're a child of God, that is all the position and title you will ever need.

Peter was a man who did not know himself. He thought more highly of himself than he should have. He had weaknesses he was not willing to admit and he was taught a few hard lessons about his real self. He thought he would never deny Christ and yet he did. This event caused him to get to know himself, and after he repented, he was restored by God and continued on to become a great apostle of Jesus. Having weaknesses and inabilities doesn't disqualify us, because God's strength is made perfect in our weaknesses, but we cannot go beyond what God enables us to do.

I recall a woman—we will call her Jane—who asked me for prayer about a troubling situation. One of her friends at work was promoted to a grade-one secretary and kept pushing Jane to also try for an upgraded position. Jane heard me preaching about becoming all you can be, and although she did not feel she had the skills to be a grade-one secretary, she felt pressured by her friend and my preaching to do so. I explained to her she needed to follow her heart and there was absolutely nothing wrong with being a grade-two secretary if that was truly where she felt God wanted her. This knowledge immediately simplified her life. She was delivered from feeling confused, and she realized she did not need to live in competition; she just needed to know and be herself.

Only Believe

"Faith is to believe what we do not see, and the reward of this faith is to see what we believe."

— St. Augustine

Jesus said to her, Did I not tell you and promise you that if you would believe and rely on Me, you would see the glory of God?

—John 11:40

Believing is the quickest way to simplify your life. Fear, doubt, unbelief, and over-reasoning complicate life, but the ability to believe removes them all. Little children simply believe what you tell them. If a child is told by his parents they will buy him a new pair of shoes on Saturday, the child does not worry all week about whether or not it will happen. They just look forward to Saturday. We should be the same way in our relationship with the Lord. We should simply believe or as the *King James translation of Mark 5:36 states, "only believe."*

Having faith and confidence that God will provide isn't always easy. Unfortunately, there isn't always a "belief button" to push to insure you will never experience doubt again. It is a growing process, and the attitude you need to have while you're waiting is just like that little child—"Saturday is coming!" Instead of giving up and getting frustrated, realize we receive the promises of God by faith and patience. Keep talking about the promise, not the problem. All the negative emotions we experience are just some of the things that complicate our lives. We don't have to get upset while we are waiting; we can choose to remain expectant and joyful. We can take the simple approach and simply believe!

The next time you feel life is so complicated you want to jump off a bridge, start saying out loud, "I believe, God!" You only have to turn to His Word to find His promises—promises assuring He will never leave you or forsake you (see Deuteronomy 31:6); promises that He is the source of every comfort and encouragement (see 2 Corinthians 1:3–4). So hold to those promises and say with conviction, "I believe, God!" You will calm down and feel ready to do whatever you need to do. You might need to say it several times, but I know from experience, believing has an amazing effect on the soul. The Bible says joy and peace are found in believing (see Romans 15:13). Any time I feel upset or sad, if I check where my belief levels are, I immediately find the source of my negative emotion. If I am willing to adjust my attitude, things get noticeably better. God keeps telling me to simplify, simplify, and then simplify some more. I am on a journey, and I hope by this point you have decided to join me. Believe and be ready to receive.

21

Regularly Reevaluate Commitments

"If you don't like something, change it; if you can't change it, change the way you think about it."

—Mary Engelbreit

Come to Me, all you who labor and are heavy-laden and overburdened, and I will cause you to rest. [I will ease and relieve and refresh your souls.]

—*Matthew 11:28*

Jesus says He wants to give us rest. He invites us to come and, perhaps, He wants to give us an opportunity to reevaluate our commitments. He wants us to find what isn't necessary and get rid of it. Anytime we feel like life has lost the simple flow it should have and, instead, has become burdensome and heavy, we should take those weights to Jesus. Life was not meant to make us feel dragged down and weary. We are not mules who spend their lives carrying a burden. We are God's children with a blood-bought right to peace and joy.

Things in life are always changing and shifting. In order to grow, we must change also, and our commitments must change to match the changes happening in our lives. My youngest daughter, Sandra, worked on our ministry staff for fifteen years. She traveled with me, was in charge of our helps ministry, and did many things she enjoyed. When she felt ready to have children, she also thought she could still work, at least part-time. Much to her surprise, she had twins and it wasn't long before she was in tears because her life was so complicated. She knew she had to make the difficult decision to not work for several years. The decision made a big difference in their family finances, and she didn't want to feel left out of things at the ministry. I respect her so much because she valued a peaceful, simple lifestyle more than money and position, and I believe God is blessing her in special ways because of her difficult decision.

I believe we often forfeit many blessings God has stored up for us because we are not willing to reevaluate commitments and cut out things that God is finished with or are no longer bearing fruit. Just because you have always done something does not mean you should always do it. We can easily get into a rut and find ourselves feeling bored and bland for no reason other than we have done too much of the same thing for too long and we need a change.

It is easy to cut things off you don't *want* to do, but what about when God asks you to lay something down your emotions are not ready to give up? What if it is something you have helped birth and build and feel attached to and even responsible for?

Would you be willing to let go of something you still enjoy, in obedience to God, in order to simplify your life? Obedience is not always easy. Much of the time it involves sacrificing our ways for God's way. Sometimes we don't understand why, but those are the times when we need to trust Him and keep moving forward. God never asks us to do anything that won't eventually make our lives better. Don't be afraid to regularly reevaluate and make changes you need to make in order to keep your life on the simple track.

22 Define Personal Priorities

"Set priorities for your goals. A major part of successful living lies in the ability to put first things first. Indeed, the reason most major goals are not achieved is that we spend our time doing second things first."

—Robert J. McKain

On the top of the heights beside the way, where the paths meet, stands Wisdom [skillful and godly]; At the gates at the entrance of the town, at the coming in at the doors she, cries out.

—Proverbs 8:2–3

Our journeys through life will bring us to many unavoidable decisions, and we will always get in trouble if we make them emotionally or according to what we think or want. God wants us to make wise decisions. When I read the verses above, I see the idea of wisdom standing at every crossroad and place of decision in our lives, calling out, "Follow me!"

I believe having wisdom is choosing to do now what we will be happy with later. That is not always easy because it may require us to sacrifice something we could easily have today for something better we can have tomorrow. Investing money is a good example. You must move some of your money to a place where you can't spend it and let it multiply over time in order to provide more money for you later on. Many people reach old age and have nothing with which to support themselves, simply because they preferred to have instant gratification throughout their lives. This is understandable, but not wise. It is a choice made mainly out of emotions. They chose what felt good at the moment and sacrificed what would have felt even better in the long-term.

In order to define personal priorities, you must realize that what someone else does may not be the right thing for you. Live your own life and be led by the Holy Spirit. Be willing to be different if that is what it takes to keep your peace and live the good life God has prearranged for you.

Priorities should have an order in your life. You should have a number one priority, number two, number three, and so on. Our first priority, for example, should always be our personal relationship with God. We should put Him into our schedule and then work everything else around Him. If we do not do this, we will find life getting more and more complicated and messy. Things can get absolutely out of control if we don't allow God to direct us.

There is no point in saying we don't have time for something, because we *make* time for whatever is important to us. If you are not doing something, it's because it isn't a priority in your life. Perhaps it does not need to be one, but if it does, then you will have to rearrange some things and get your priorities in line. We don't just get them straight once and never need to adjust them again. It is something we must do quite frequently.

There are a great many things clamoring for our attention in life, and it is rather easy to get off track—to get our priorities out-of-order. The answer to this problem of out-of-control priorities is simple, if we take the time to ask the right questions. What are your priorities? Make a list of what's truly important to you and use that list to help you in your day-to-day decision making. You will simplify when you prioritize.

23 Choose Your Battles

"In the long run, we shape our lives, and we shape ourselves. The process never ends until we die. And the choices we make are ultimately our own responsibility."

—ELEANOR ROOSEVELT

You shall not need to fight in this battle; take your positions, stand still, and see the deliverance of the Lord [Who is] with you, O Judah and Jerusalem.

—2 Chronicles 20:17

Quite often, the simple life feels out of reach because of all the problems and challenges that crop up. Trials and difficulties will happen, but it's *how* we handle them that makes the difference. There are far too many battles in life to try and fight them all, so we must choose the ones we feel are worth the effort. Many things are better off left alone. Prayer and time also changes a lot of things, and just waiting for a while may save us a battle or two. If you are confronted with a challenge, don't respond right away. Give yourself time to think about it, and wait a couple of days to decide. Take the time to weigh your choices so you can make wise, solid decisions.

God told Jehoshaphat (see 2 Chronicles 20:17–22) that he and his people did not need to fight the battle at hand, yet there were other times He did instruct His people to fight. We need to listen to God and choose our battles carefully. I lived for many years making a battle out of everything. I prided myself in being a confronter, but I finally realized it often takes more courage to wait on God than it does to attack something in my own timing.

God told Jehoshaphat to worship, to sing, to praise, and to wait. As he obeyed God, the enemy became confused and destroyed each other. Are you in the habit of praying and thinking before you attack, or do you just attack and wonder why life gets so complex and frustrating? Do you ever wonder why you are always dealing with something? If so, maybe you need to simply not deal with everything that comes along. Some things work themselves out if you give them time to do so. Ask God for the wisdom to recognize the difference between problems that have the potential to blaze and those that will likely smolder and burn themselves out.

24

Be Quick to Forgive

"Forgiveness doesn't make the other person right,
it makes you free."

—STORMIE OMARTIAN

*For if you forgive people their trespasses [their reckless
and willful sins, leaving them, letting them go, and
giving up resentment], your heavenly Father will also
forgive you.*

—*Matthew 6:14*

One of the quickest ways to complicate your life is to be easily offended and hold grudges. God tells us in His Word to be quick to forgive (see James 1:19) for a reason. He wants us to enjoy peace, and that is impossible if we are bitter, resentful, and angry. Refusing to forgive is like an acid that destroys the container it is in.

God is our Vindicator, and He promises to deal with our enemies if we trust Him to do so. He says we should pray for those who hurt us instead of being angry at them; and when we do, it releases God to deal with the person who has wronged us. We actually do ourselves a favor when we forgive because it releases us from a prison of inner turmoil and greatly simplifies our life. If we are confused and upset inside, it affects our daily life in a negative way.

I have decided I just don't have the time or the energy to be angry. I want to enjoy my life, and I cannot do that if I let other people's choices control my attitudes. I encourage you to make a decision right now that you will be quick to forgive. The sooner you forgive a person after they hurt you, the easier it is to do the next time. Don't allow anger to fester in your heart and become a root of bitterness which will contaminate not only you but others around you.

By allowing ourselves to remain angry, we end up taking our anger out on people who have nothing to do with the original offense. I spent years being bitter because my father abused me, and I usually took it out on my husband, Dave, who had nothing at all to do with it. God taught me to stop trying to collect from someone who didn't owe me anything.

When we are hurt, trying to collect what we are owed from the wrong person is not the answer. God promises to pay us back and actually give us double blessings for our former trouble if we will do things His way (see Isaiah 61:7). God forgives us for all our sins on a regular basis, and He expects us to do the same for others.

By choosing to forgive, your feelings toward the individual who hurt you will not necessarily change immediately. I believe if I do what I can do, then God will do what I cannot do. I can make a choice to obey God's Word, but only God can change the way I feel. Our feelings always catch up with our choices if we give them a little time.

25

Mind Your Own Business

"I remember that a wise friend of mine did usually say 'That which is everybody's business is nobody's business.'"

—Izaac Walton

Set a guard, O Lord, before my mouth; keep watch at the door of my lips.

—Psalm 141:3

The Bible is filled with practical advice for everyday life. One of the things it instructs us to do is mind our own business (see 1 Thessalonians 4:11). Needing to express an opinion about almost everything and everyone is a symptom of pride and always leads to relationship problems.

One time my husband and I were discussing a man who lived in a rather large house in our neighborhood. We were expressing our opinion about him being single and wondering why he wanted all that space to himself. We assumed he purchased it for an investment, but we thought maybe he would have been better off investing in the stock market instead of taking on such a large home to care for. God was dealing with me at the time about learning to mind my own business, and suddenly I realized Dave and I were driving down the street discussing the finances of a man we didn't even know. Once I saw how ridiculous that was, it helped me also see how often we have opinions about things which really don't concern us at all.

We all have enough business of our own to take care of without getting involved in other people's business. If you have a tendency to be opinionated, make an effort to pray people will follow God and then don't worry about what they are doing.

I often say to myself, "Joyce, that is none of your business." I find that often helps me stay on track with my attitude. If you really stop and think about it logically, what sense does it make to have an opinion about something having nothing to do with you? It makes no sense, and just keeps us busy doing something that will never bear any good fruit. Make a decision to obey God's Word and forget about the business of others. You'll be amazed at how much lighter you'll feel.

26 Be Merciful

"The unthankful heart discovers no mercies; but the thankful heart will find, in every hour, some heavenly blessings."

—HARRIET BEECHER STOWE

The merciful, kind, and generous man benefits himself [for his deeds return to bless him], but he who is cruel and callous [to the wants of others] brings on himself retribution.

—*Proverbs 11:17*

Another way to simplify your life, increase your peace, and improve relationships is to be merciful. God tells us in His Word to put on behavior that is marked by "tenderhearted pity *and* mercy" (Colossians 3:12). We are to be kind, long-suffering, and ready to forgive. Being hard-hearted, legalistic, and rigid only makes us miserable and does not win us friends.

Mercy cannot be deserved; it is a gift given to one who does not deserve it. God is merciful and it is because of His great mercy we are not consumed by our own sin (see Lamentations 3:22). God never expects us to give away something we do not have, so He gives us mercy first and then expects us to let it flow through us to other people. Be a giver and be generous in mercy!

If we don't make the decision to be merciful then we have no option but to be angry most of the time. The fact is, people are not perfect and everywhere you go you will find they make mistakes. We must all realize that not only do we have to deal with people who are irritating, but they also have to deal with us. We rarely see ourselves the way others do. We may think we are the perfect example of how a person should be, but I can assure you, it's not true. The Bible actually says we judge others for the same things we do (see Romans 2:1). We look at ourselves through rose-colored glasses, but we look at others through a magnifying glass. There is always an excuse for our wrong behavior, but for other people, there is no excuse!

Showing mercy means showing compassion and heartfelt concern for others. It doesn't always come easy for everyone, but it is important just the same. Mercy makes the soul meek; by reaching out to other people, we remind ourselves how good it is to find mercy.

When we make an effort to have a merciful attitude, not only do we please God, we save ourselves a lot of turmoil. God's ways are simple and peaceful, and He says to be merciful even as He is merciful. It may not always seem fair to show mercy when you feel someone deserves judgment, but God's ways always bring a reward in the end.

27

Don't Be Judgmental

"If you judge people, you have no time to love them."

—MOTHER TERESA

[My] brethren, do not speak evil about or accuse one another. He that maligns a brother or judges his brother is maligning and criticizing the Law and judging the Law. But if you judge the Law, you are not a practicer of the Law but a censor and judge [of it].

—James 4:11

When we judge someone, we pass sentence upon them and only God has the right to do that. One definition I've heard says that judgment is setting oneself up as God. I don't think any of us really want that job, do we? It is very easy to glance at someone or at a situation and quickly judge without really knowing anything at all. God not only knows what someone is doing, He knows why they are doing it. We judge according to the flesh, but God sees the heart.

Jesus told those who were ready to stone the woman caught in adultery that whoever among them was without sin could throw the first stone. After they took time to consider what He said, they all dropped their rocks at their feet and left, one by one. Who among us can say we have no sin? How then can we be so quick to judge other people for their mistakes? We can judge sin, but we cannot judge the heart of a person. The more we study God's Word, the quicker we will recognize wrongdoing, but we must not let that turn into a habit of judging everyone who does not do what they should be doing. Once again, we need to follow God's Word and "watch and pray." Don't watch and judge, but watch and pray! Treat others the way you want to be treated and watch life get sweeter.

Each time we judge, whether for good or for bad, we sow a seed that produces a harvest in our own lives. If we are critical and merciless, we will be judged in the same way, but if we give mercy we will reap mercy. We have the ability to love people and should do so because that is the one commandment Jesus left. He said, "Just as I have loved you, so you too should love one another" (John 13:34; see also John 15:12).

Being quick to judge is another symptom of pride, and the Bible teaches us that pride always comes before destruction and downfall, but humility preceeds honor (see Proverbs 18:12). If we want trouble, we can continue being judgmental, but if we want honor we can have a humble attitude. The choice is ours.

28

Be Decisive

"The most decisive actions of our life—I mean those that are most likely to decide the whole course of our future—are, more often than not, unconsidered."

—Andre Gide

I appeal to you therefore, brethren, and beg of you in view of [all] the mercies of God, to make a decisive dedication of your bodies [presenting all your members and faculties] as a living sacrifice, holy (devoted, consecrated) and well pleasing to God, which is your reasonable (rational, intelligent) service and spiritual worship.

—*Romans 12:1*

Indecision is a miserable place to be and certainly not a fruit of the simple life. Simplicity prays, seeks wisdom, and decides. There is no waffling. It sticks with the decision it made unless there is a very good reason to change it. The apostle James said the double-minded man is unstable in all of his ways and will not receive anything he asks from the Lord. How can God give us anything if we can never make up our minds concerning what we want?

Insecure people have difficulty making decisions because they are always afraid they will make the wrong one. They have a low opinion of themselves and don't trust themselves to do the right thing. Perfectionists also have difficulty because they never want to take a chance on being wrong. Anyone who is decisive occasionally makes a bad decision, but they make more right ones than wrong ones. I always say you cannot drive a parked car. Some people have had their life in park for so long, they have lost all sense of direction and feel confused about everything. God has only one gear—forward. It is not backward and it is certainly not park! Sometimes we need to do something just to keep from continuing to do nothing.

Do the best you can to make a wise decision and trust God to cover you if you make mistakes. He sees your heart and never expects more than the best you know how to do. As you make decisions and go forward in life, you will gain experience. Sometimes you learn what you have done is right and other times you learn not to ever do that particular thing again because it turned out badly. It's okay if things don't end with a perfect result. No child ever learns how to walk without falling down multiple times. They would never learn if they just sat and cried about the fall; they must get up and try again and again. Pretty soon, the walking that gave them such a hard time progresses to running.

Make a decision today to be more decisive. You will discover how much of life's clutter you'll cut out and will soon be running with progress instead of indecisively going nowhere.

29 Think Before You Speak

Before you speak ask yourself if what you are going to say is true, is kind, is necessary, is helpful. If the answer is no, maybe what you are about to say should be left unsaid.

—Bernard Meltzer

He who guards his mouth keeps his life, but he who opens wide his lips comes to ruin.

—*Proverbs 13:3*

I have caused a lot of complicated messes in my life by not thinking before I spoke. Over the years, I have made progress and gained wisdom in this area, but I still make mistakes and constantly have to remind myself to THINK BEFORE I SPEAK!

The tongue is an unruly evil according to the book of James (see James 3:8). It is the spark from which so many problems often develop, and if we don't get it under control, we often see the equivalent of a forest fire in its wake. Words are containers for power, but they carry and deliver the negative as well as the positive. If we speak from the flesh rather than the spirit, the power delivered will be negative. The writer of Proverbs wrote that life and death are in the power of the tongue (see Proverbs 18:21). That is a strong statement and should be seriously considered.

Every kind of beast can be tamed, but the tongue cannot be tamed without the help of God. We must listen carefully to the promptings of the Holy Spirit within us and stop talking the moment we get a signal we are going in the wrong direction. Better yet, don't even start talking until we get the go-ahead from God. There are many times I want to talk to my husband about something but get a feeling down deep inside that it is just not the right time. For years, I ignored that feeling and did my talking when I felt like it; and for all of those years my mouth caused complicated problems for my life. I have made a commitment to listen more and speak less, but I must admit, I need help. How about you pray for me and I will pray for you as you read this book? We will believe together that we will have the grace from God to listen to wisdom (God) and think before we speak.

30

Be a God Pleaser

"The safest place to be is in the will of God."

—ANONYMOUS

*Now am I trying to win the favor of men, or of God? Do I seek
to please men? If I were still seeking popularity with men,
I should not be a bond servant of Christ (the Messiah).*

—Galatians 1:10

In the verse above, the apostle Paul says if he was trying to be popular with people, he would not have become an apostle of the Lord Jesus Christ. The pressure to please people will build a wall keeping us from pleasing God and fulfilling our God-ordained destiny.

It's normal to want acceptance. Most of us experience rejection early in life from some source. It doesn't matter who it's from—parents, siblings, teachers, or peers—it always hurts and the painful memory causes us to do almost anything to avoid it in the future. The fear of rejection causes us to react emotionally instead of wisely. Wisdom always does now what it will be satisfied with later on in life, but emotions do what feels good right now. They push us to do whatever it takes to avoid pain and discomfort.

For years I let people control me, but eventually I

discovered they really did not care about me. They were using me to make them happy, but had no interest in my joy. When I received the call from God to be in ministry, all the people I thought were my friends rejected me without hesitation. I was no longer doing what they approved of, so I was no longer necessary in their lives. I was deeply hurt and felt very much alone, but I am grateful God gave me the grace to choose Him over them.

I shudder to think I might still be living a phony life of pretense, trying to win the favor of people who really did not genuinely care about me. People who are real friends will help you be all God wants you to be. They won't use you and then discard you when you no longer please them. Trying to please all of the people all of the time will really complicate your life because everyone seems to expect something different. When you spend so much time and energy trying to please others, you take a great risk in losing yourself. Always remember God must be number one in your life. Even if everyone else walks away from you, He promises to never leave you or forsake you.

31   Don't Receive Condemnation

"Compassion will cure more sins than condemnation."

—Henry Ward Beecher

Therefore, [there is] now no condemnation (no adjudging guilty of wrong) for those who are in Christ Jesus, who live [and] walk not after the dictates of the flesh, but after the dictates of the Spirit.

—*Romans 8:1*

Condemnation is a feeling of guilt and shame that presses you down. That is why people often refer to being "under" condemnation. For example, one might say, "Jane got her dates mixed up and failed to show up for the field trip at school; now she is under condemnation. She has felt guilty and ashamed ever since it happened."

Jesus comes to lift us up, not press us down. It is the devil who wants to press us down and keep us there. He brings condemnation, but Jesus offers forgiveness and restoration. The devil offers complexity and confusion; Jesus offers simplicity in its purest form. Every time we sin, the Holy Spirit convicts us but the devil tries to denounce and condemn us. We need to know the difference. Conviction is for the purpose of leading us to admit our sin and repent.

Condemnation only makes us feel guilty and actually weakens us and keeps us in the cycle of sin.

We must decide not to accept condemnation. You would not take arsenic if someone offered it to you, so why take condemnation when the Bible plainly teaches that we have been set free from it through Jesus Christ? He paid the price for our sins by dying on the cross and rising from the dead. If we believe in Him and look to Him as our Savior, we are free from the power of sin (see Romans 6:7–8), which I believe is condemnation.

Since we do sin and make mistakes, there is no hope of life being simple if our destiny is to succumb to condemnation, pressure, and guilt each time we fail. Thank God He has set us free through Jesus Christ and offers us a simple life filled with peace and joy. It is already available; all you need to do is believe and receive!

32

Refuse to Live in Fear

"Courage is resistance to fear, mastery of fear,
not absence of fear."

—MARK TWAIN

*The Lord is my Light and my Salvation—whom shall I fear or
dread? The Lord is the Refuge and Stronghold of my life—of
whom shall I be afraid?*

—*Psalm 27:1*

There is certainly nothing simple about fear. It torments and prevents progress and is a major obstacle Satan uses against people to keep them out of God's will. There is quite a bit people tend to fear. They are afraid of other people, the past, the future, going without, sacrifice, heights, elevators, water, germs. If you can think of it, someone is afraid of it. We may feel fear but we do not have to give in to it. We can do whatever we need and want to do, even if we have to "do it afraid." Courage is not the absence of fear, but it is taking action in the presence of fear.

Anytime God leads us to do something, He always supplies everything we need for the task. He gives us the ability, help, finances, courage, wisdom, and everything else that's required to finish well. We may not feel or see those provisions right away, but as we step out in faith, those things will always be present. Satan uses fear to cause us to shrink back, but God wants us to go all the way through and see our dreams fulfilled.

As I pursued a simple life, God made it obvious to me not to spend a lot of time with people who were extremely fearful. We cannot win our battles when we are surrounded by fear. Gideon was headed to war and God told him the first thing he needed to do was get rid of all the soldiers who were afraid, and that was about two-thirds of them (see Judges 7:3). I am not suggesting we reject people who experience fear, but I am saying if we want to accomplish the will of God, we need people around us who understand the nature of fear and refuse to be ruled by it.

Fear clouds our thinking, torments us emotionally, causes us to act irrationally, and in general complicates *everything*. It is time to say no to fear. God has not given us a spirit of fear, but of power, love, and a sound mind (see 2 Timothy 1:7).

33

Follow Your Heart

"Profound joy of the heart is like a magnet that indicates the path of life. One has to follow it, even though one enters into a way full of difficulties."

—MOTHER TERESA

In Whom, because of our faith in Him, we dare to have the boldness (courage and confidence) of free access (an unreserved approach to God with freedom and without fear).

—*Ephesians 3:12*

You are probably familiar with the statement, "To thine own heart be true." One of the ways we make our lives so complex is when we veer off course and ignore what is really important to us. If we put aside our own hearts and follow what the world thinks we should and ought to do, we will find ourselves unfulfilled and empty. Life will be tasteless. We will go through the motions, but nothing will satisfy us. What do you want out of life? What do you believe God's will is for you? Some people spend so much time meeting what they think their obligations are that they don't even know what *they* want. They never ask themselves because they figure it is way out of reach.

When I ask what you want out of life, I am not

talking about selfish desire; I am talking about heart desire. There is something deep in your heart God has planted there. Everyone is called and equipped to do something, and that includes you! It takes boldness to follow your heart instead of the crowd. When God called me to teach His Word, it was not popular at all for women to do that. I lost my friends, and even family members rejected me as a rebel who was deceived and misguided. I didn't have a very good reputation among the people in our community, but then, neither did Jesus. It is still a wonder to me that I found the courage to follow God rather than the crowd. I think I was so fed up with "life as usual," I was willing to do something radical if it took that for me to feel satisfied inside.

It is certainly not simple to have dreams and visions in your heart that you ignore and constantly try to push down while you simultaneously try to make yourself enjoy doing something you actually hate. You might think it will complicate your life if you end up making some people angry in order to follow your heart, but the truth is, following your heart is absolutely necessary if you ever really intend to enjoy a simple life of hearty obedience to God.

34

Don't Be Afraid of What People Think

"A man's reputation is what other people think of him; his character is what he really is."

—John Milton

Then the cares and anxieties of the world and distractions of the age, and the pleasure and delight and false glamour and deceitfulness of riches, and the craving and passionate desire for other things creep in and choke and suffocate the Word, and it becomes fruitless.

—*Mark 4:19*

Being excessively concerned about what other people think is an open door to torment. Of course, we all enjoy being well thought of, but it is not possible to be liked by everyone all the time. Someone is going to think something negative about you and there is nothing you can do about it. If it isn't one person, it will be another. But then again, sometimes we worry about what people think and the truth is they are not thinking about us at all.

The Bible says we should cast all of our cares upon God for He cares for us (see 1 Peter 5:7), and that includes the care of what people think. I can only live my life to please God and if people are not satisfied, then they will have to take it up with God, not with me. If I try to please both God and people, life gets too complicated and I get confused and frustrated. I experienced rejection at first when I decided to live to please God, but after a while, God gave me new friends who were pursuing the same thing I was, and together we stand against the fear of what people think.

In God's economy, we usually have to be willing to lose something we have in order to gain what we really want. Why hang on to something that is never going to satisfy you anyway? Don't live under the tyranny of what people think. Stop trying to convince them of your good intentions and let them think what they want to think. God is your defender; He will vindicate you in due time.

What can someone's thoughts do to you anyway? Why live your life being afraid of a thought? God has not given us His Holy Spirit so we can be in bondage to fear (see Romans 8:15). Make the choice to care about what God thinks more than anyone else and it will simplify much in your life.

35

Keep the Strife out
of Your Life

"Heat and Animosity, contest and conflict, may sharpen
the wits, although they rarely do; they never strengthen
the understanding, clear the perspicacity, guide the
judgment, or improve the heart."

—WALTER SAVAGE LANDOR

*It is an honor for a man to cease from strife and keep aloof
from it, but every fool will quarrel.*

—*Proverbs 20:3*

When we talk about strife, we're talking about all
of the bickering, arguing, heated disagreement, and
angry undercurrents. We can experience strife with
friends, family, and the day-to-day tasks of life. The
Bible teaches us the servant of the Lord must not
get caught up in strife (see 2 Timothy 2:23–24). It
says we are to have nothing to do with trifling, (ill-
informed, unedifying, stupid) controversies over
ignorant questionings, because they foster strife and
breed quarrels.

To keep conflict and discord out of our lives, we
must be willing to avoid conversations that lead to
distress and turmoil. I can tell when Dave and I are
having a conversation that is becoming a bit heated.

I often choose to just drop it because, on those occasions, what we are debating is, often, something not worth arguing about. It may even be something we are not well informed enough to be discussing anyway.

Our human desire to be right often leads us to a great deal of strife. In order to keep dissension and disputes out of your life, entertain the idea that even though you really think you are right, there is a possibility you are wrong. Being right is highly overrated anyway. We cause all kinds of problems just by trying to prove we are right, and what good does it really do in the end? It satisfies the flesh, but God has called us to peace.

Let's go back to that definition of strife: arguing, bickering, heated conversations, and an angry undercurrent. All this makes me feel life is really complicated, but peace is simple and sweet. Strife blocks our blessings and opens the door for all kinds of trouble. Strife weakens us, but agreement increases our power. As the old saying goes, "United we stand, divided we fall."

The next time you have an argument with someone, stop and ask yourself if what you're discussing is actually worth losing your peace over.

36

Be Positive

"A pessimist sees the difficulty in every opportunity;
an optimist sees the opportunity in every difficulty."

—Sir Winston Churchill

*And be constantly renewed in the spirit of your mind [having a
fresh mental and spiritual attitude].*

—*Ephesians 4:23*

Being positive is a choice. It is an attitude we decide to live with and it opens the door for God to work in our lives. However, we also have the choice to be the opposite—we can be negative and open a door to allow the devil to work. When the atmosphere is filled with negativity, it leaves a heavy feeling and a burden we do not need to bear. Even if your situation seems negative, being negative about it is not going to help correct it. Is your problem really your problem, or is it the way you view your problem?

As soon as we allow the negative to slant our viewpoint and become our filter for everything, we lose our joy and our peace. A negative person is not going to get answers from God so they feel confused about what to do and everything goes from bad to worse. Why not help yourself and everyone around you by deciding to look on the bright side?

Joyce Meyer

For many years of my life, I was a very negative person. I was raised in a negative environment, and out of ignorance, I merely continued in what I had always known. I can tell you my life was not enjoyable. It was anything but simple, because I took my challenges in life and made them a lot worse with a bad attitude. It seemed I always had problems and all I did was complain about everything, which only increased the intensity of my problems. Only when I finally started focusing on the positive and releasing the negative did my world settle down and allow peace to return.

You can change the atmosphere you live in from negative to positive beginning right now. God is waiting to answer a lot of those prayers you have prayed, and He needs you to live with an attitude of faith. Have a talk with yourself and be reminded that being negative does not do any good, so why waste your time on something that is useless? Concentrate on the bright side of life and you will be amazed at all the good you can find.

Stop Doing Things You Don't Do Well

"Do what you're good at and everything else will fall into place."

—Willnett Crockett

In all your ways know, recognize, and acknowledge Him, and He will direct and make straight and plain your paths.

—*Proverbs 3:6*

Do you find yourself trying to keep up with everyone else you know when it comes to talent and ability? Ever find yourself falling short with some of those things? Any person desiring to simplify their life must learn to give at least 80 percent of their time to their top two or three strengths and stop wasting time doing things they don't do well. We are all encouraged by accomplishment; therefore, if we keep doing what makes us feel like a failure, we won't have the encouragement we need to enjoy our lives.

You don't have to do something well just because someone you know does it well. My neighbor was the perfect homemaker. She made her family's clothes, had a garden, was a great decorator and cook; she could have been an equal with Martha Stewart. I, on the other hand, could not sew, had no garden, and was, at best, an average cook. I attempted a garden but hated it. I tried to sew and hated it even worse than the garden. I was miserable and life seemed very complicated because I spent every day doing things I hated just so I could feel like I was a "normal woman."

God had to teach me that even though I was not like my neighbor, it did not mean something was wrong with me. I had to be bold enough to stop doing things I did not do well and stop worrying about what people thought. If we were all good at the same thing, a lot of needs in this world would never be met. God equips each of us in a different way, and it is by working together, each with our own strengths and talents, that we accomplish His will.

38

Don't Worry about Your Children

"When I approach a child, he inspires in me two sentiments; tenderness for what he is, and respect for what he may become."

—Louis Pasteur

And who of you by worrying and being anxious can add one unit of measure (cubit) to his stature or to the span of his life?

—Matthew 6:27

Some people feel if they don't worry about their children, they are not good parents; however, the Bible teaches us worry is not God's will and is useless. I believe worry is like rocking in a rocking chair. It keeps you busy, but gets you nowhere.

Do the best job you can to raise your children according to godly principles and leave the rest to God! When we worry, we show we don't really trust God. We need to pray for our children and then cast our care on God.

I have four grown children who are all serving God, but I sure wasted a lot of time worrying when they were growing up. I wondered if a couple of them could even survive if they left home, but to my surprise, they did very well. Your children may be capable of more than you think they are. Don't be afraid to let them spread their wings and try to fly solo at the right time.

Like most parents we had some kind of issue with each of our children. Two of them struggled getting through school, one was very messy, and another was an extreme perfectionist and put tremendous pressure on herself. The good news is they all made it and are doing fine. Some of them took a little detour and made some bad choices, but they learned from them and came full circle back to what they were taught. God's Word states that if we train them in the way they should go, when they are old they will not depart from it (see Proverbs 22:6).

If you are concerned about one of your children, just cling to that promise I just mentioned. Worrying will only make you feel confused and complicate your life. It will not help your children, so why not put the energy you normally use on worry into believing God and watch Him work on your behalf?

Avoid Excessive Reasoning

"Time makes more converts than reason."

—Thomas Paine

Lean on, trust in, and be confident in the Lord with all your heart and mind and do not rely on your own insight or understanding.

—*Proverbs 3:5*

God's Word teaches us not to rely on our own understanding. That simply means we don't need to waste our time trying to figure out things only God knows. This doesn't mean we aren't supposed to think about things, but it does mean we're not supposed to obsess over the challenges and conflicts that come day by day. God invites us to simplify our lives by trusting Him and living in faith, but trust always means we have some unanswered questions in our lives. If we knew everything, we wouldn't need God! Admit you don't know everything and don't worry about it. It is not your job to have all the answers; it is your job to trust God to provide answers at the exact right time.

During a desperate moment of realizing I needed to simplify my life, one of the first things I had to give up was reasoning. My mind had to be simple if my life was going to be simple. I had to stop analyzing and fretting over things I shouldn't. Constantly revolving my mind around and around every issue, trying to come up with an answer that made sense, was certainly not simple. I felt mentally worn out most of the time and a lot of what I thought I figured out turned out to be wrong anyway. God showed me I was addicted to reasoning. I could not settle down and feel peaceful until I thought I had everything in life figured out. I had to be weaned off reasoning much like a baby has to be weaned off a pacifier.

I eventually made the decision to stop trying to figure things out, but it took a while for my flesh to settle down and feel peaceful when I had unanswered questions. Each time I started to feel confused, I knew I had slipped into my old habit and I would say out loud, "God, I trust You and I refuse to get into reasoning." Gradually, I was completely delivered from what I call "the need to know." I am now comfortable not knowing because I know God and He knows everything. He will also let me know if and when I need to know, so in the meantime I can rest in His love and know He is in control. This process took time to develop in my life, but it has been worth it. If you are someone who tries to figure out too much, I suggest you start today in breaking your addiction to reasoning and learn to trust the Master Reasoner, God Himself!

40 Have Simple Friends

"Some people come into our lives and quickly go. Some stay for a while and leave footprints on our hearts. And we are never, ever the same."

—Anonymous

Make no friendships with a man given to anger, and with a wrathful man do not associate.

—*Proverbs 22:24*

The people we spend time with affect us, so it stands to reason, if we want a more simple life, we should not have a lot of complicated people for close friends. If I am around people who are very intense and always stressed out, they get me stressed; but if I am around people who are peaceful, it helps me remain peaceful too. When I am around people who are lighthearted and thoroughly enjoy even the very simple things in life, it reminds me to do the same.

Having a close relationship with a person who is extremely insecure can be complicated. You find yourself always taking care not to hurt their feelings, instead of being free to be yourself and enjoy being around your friends. Likewise, negative people are not easy to be around. They resemble dark clouds everywhere they go.

Not everyone understands the importance of choosing friends wisely. They merely get involved with whoever is in their space, and quite often those choices are the source of a lot of their problems. Some people could drastically change the quality of their life just by changing who they spend time with.

I have had enough complication in my lifetime, and I don't want to spend my leisure time with a person who seems to complicate every plan, conversation, and hour we try to spend together. Take an inventory of your friendships, and if they are not nurturing you, then consider making some changes.

41

Find the Most Efficient Way to Do Things

"The men who succeed are the **efficient** few. They are the few who have the ambition and will power to develop themselves."

—Robert Burton

Behave yourselves wisely [living prudently and with discretion] in your relations with those of the outside world (the non-Christians), making the very most of the time and seizing (buying up) the opportunity.

—*Colossians 4:5*

I can remember a time in my life when I would spend days and lots of gas trying to get a pair of shoes on sale. I thought I was being frugal by searching for the ones on sale, but it finally dawned on me, I was wasting more time and money than I was saving. We often forget that for most of us, time is money. If you waste your time, you are wasting one of the most precious gifts God has given you. Once time is used, we never get it back, so we should spend it wisely.

For example, learn to combine errands. You may think you're doing well because you're doing everything the moment you think of it and not procrastinating, but when it comes to errands, that is not always the best strategy. Plot out a route that doesn't waste time and gas, and set aside a specific time each week to go where you need to. It will help you not feel so frazzled. If you feel like you are constantly running around all over the place, maybe you are!

I have recently started writing down phone calls I need to make and setting aside specific times to make all my phone calls for that day. It keeps me from feeling like I am on the phone every few minutes. I realize some calls cannot wait, but a lot of them can. Also, remember you do not have to take every call that comes in on your phone. Technology today enables us to know most of the time who is calling, and it may be someone you can call back later when you make your phone calls. This will help you feel you are ordering your day instead of it ordering you.

There are many ways to save time, and we need to take the time to look for them. Think about what you have been doing recently and see if you can creatively come up with ways to be more efficient. This will give you a great start to achieving a simple life.

42 | Be Thankful

"No duty is more urgent than that of returning thanks."
—ANONYMOUS

I will give to the Lord the thanks due to His rightness and
justice, and I will sing praise to the name of the Lord
Most High.

—*Psalm 7:17*

Being thankful and saying so helps us take the more simple approach to life. We can all find plenty to complain about if we look for it, but if it does no good, why do it? God tells us in His Word not to complain, find fault, or murmur about anything (see Philippians 2:14). He actually says that when we do grumble and gripe, in reality, we are finding fault with Him.

The apostle Paul teaches we should not be anxious about anything, but in all things by prayer and petition, with thanksgiving, we should let our requests be made known unto God and only then the peace that passes understanding shall be ours (see Philippians 4:6–7). I remember a time when I asked God to give me something and His response was there was no point in giving me something else to complain about. He showed me no matter what I had, I always found a way to complain about what I did not have. I have worked since that time to count my blessings and voice my gratitude.

Having a thankful heart shows God we are ready for a new level of blessings. Thanksgiving is part of the lifestyle of one who genuinely worships and praises God. Complaining all week then going to church and singing a few songs on Sunday and calling it worship does not make it so. I don't want to merely worship. I want to be a worshiper who worships God in spirit and truth, which is His will (see John 4:24).

An attitude of gratitude certainly helps to simplify life. It keeps our mind free for thoughts that minister peace and joy, rather than turmoil. It also keeps our conversation going in a direction that creates a positive atmosphere everyone can enjoy.

43

Count the Cost Before You Commit

"He who is most slow in making a promise is the most faithful in performance of it."

—Jean-Jacques Rousseau

But above all [things], my brethren, do not swear, either by heaven or by earth or by any other oath; but let your yes be [a simple] yes, and your no be [a simple] no, so that you may not sin and fall under condemnation.

—James 5:12

It is very unwise to say yes to a commitment without really considering all the aspects of what it will require, and yet, thinking through something before we commit is rarely done. Something can sound exciting on Monday, but unless it is something we are sold out on and ready to invest ourselves in, by Friday it is drudgery.

Many people complicate their lives greatly because they say yes to too many things without counting the cost of what they'll be giving up or what they'll be adding to their already full plate. Often we speak out of emotions and then wish later we would have kept quiet. Sad to say, wishing changes nothing. If we want change, we must change the way we do things.

Do you really want to make the high car payment for five years just to have a newer model when the automobile you have is paid for and serving you well? Anyone can greatly simplify life by slowing down and actually thinking about what they are about to get themselves into. Before you make a major commitment, walk away and get by yourself for a few minutes. Let your emotions subside and then decide. If the desire stays and you feel it is right, then do it; otherwise, keep your life simple and avoid overcommitting.

44

Pray about Everything

"Pray, and let God worry."

—Martin Luther

Pray at all times (on every occasion, in every season) in the Spirit, with all [manner of] prayer and entreaty. To that end keep alert and watch with strong purpose and perseverance, interceding in behalf of all the saints (God's consecrated people).

—*Ephesians 6:18*

The more we try to do things on our own without asking God to get involved, the more complicated life will be. We need His blessing on *everything* we do and the way to get it is to pray. First, we should pray about whether or not we should even be doing what we are about to do and if we are, we need to depend on God to help us do it. All too often, we just decide we want to do something and then we wonder why it is such a struggle.

Jesus is the Author and Finisher of our faith, but He is not obligated to finish anything He did not start. Jesus said He did nothing independent of His Father (see John 5:30), and we should follow His example.

God's grace is His ability coming to us free of

charge which helps us do with ease what we could never do on our own with any amount of struggle or human effort. Whether you're attempting a new diet, going on an exercise program, making a career change, getting married, or taking on anything else, remember to pray about it. You and God are partners in life, so don't forfeit your partner's help because you fail to ask Him for it. James said, "You have not because you ask not" (see James 4:2).

Ask for God's help and watch Him answer.

45 Don't Fret over Evildoers

"I believe God is managing affairs and that He doesn't need any advice from me. With God in charge, I believe everything will work out for the best in the end. So what is there to worry about?"

—HENRY FORD

Fret not yourself because of evildoers, neither be envious against those who work unrighteousness (that which is not upright or in right standing with God).

—Psalm 37:1

Paul told Timothy that in the last days, times would be very difficult and hard to bear because people would be selfish, lovers of money, abusive, rebellious, proud, and arrogant (see 2 Timothy 3:1). Friends, we are living in those times Paul talked about. You may have had certain people come to mind when you read those words. These days, it would certainly be very easy to fret over numerous things, including those kinds of people, but God tells us not to fret over evildoers, but to trust Him and keep doing good (see Psalm 37).

Life gets very complicated if we don't stay focused on the right thing. Our tendency is to focus on the problem at hand, but what we really need to do is focus on completing God's will. Sometimes I get very weary of listening to people talk about all the problems in our world today. I think we should talk about what we can do to make it a better place, not just what is wrong with it. I am not suggesting we ignore the problems, but rather than fretting over them, let's look for solutions.

Jesus had problems in His day but He focused on obeying God and helping people. God will take care of the evildoers in due time. He says that soon we will look where they used to be and they will be gone (see Psalm 37:10). Sometimes it appears those who do evil actually fare better than good people, and that is frustrating and confusing. But, God promises in the end, the meek will inherit the earth (see Psalm 37:11). I refuse to spend my time being frustrated about someone else's bad decisions. I still believe there are more good things in the world than bad, and I am committed to looking for those things and talking about them.

46

Trust God to Change You

"You can't change circumstances and you can't change other people, but God can change you."

—Evelyn A. Theissen

But by the grace (the unmerited favor and blessing) of God I am what I am, and His grace toward me was not [found to be] for nothing (fruitless and without effect). In fact, I worked harder than all of them [the apostles], though it was not really I, but the grace (the unmerited favor and blessing) of God which was with me.

—1 Corinthians 15:10

Do you ever struggle with yourself? Do you see things about yourself you know need to change and desperately try to change them? I did that for many years and they were some of the most complicated and frustrating years of my life. I finally saw, through God's grace, how it was a waste of time for me to try to fix something only God could do something about.

Paul wrote that God has begun a good work in us and He will complete it and bring it to its finish (see Philippians 1:6). I try to remember God did not invite me into the game, throw me the ball, and tell me to make the touchdown by myself. We receive everything we need the same way we received Jesus: by believing. The only thing we receive by struggle and effort is frustration. I remember putting a sign on my refrigerator that said, "Frustration = works of the flesh." God has graciously taught me each time I feel frustrated, it is because I was taking over and trying to do something without His help. It is what His Word calls "works of the flesh" and is something He hates. We honor God when we depend on Him in all things.

When God shows us something that is wrong with us, all He wants us to do is agree with Him and repent. I recommend you tell Him you cannot change unless He helps you and that you thank Him daily that He is doing so. You may not see results at first, but faith works. A person living by faith begins by believing what they do not see or feel, and they get results as they continue believing and waiting patiently. Stop wrestling with yourself and believe that God is working in you right now and that you will see the results. God can change you for the better and for good.

47

Trust God to Change
Other People

"Trust the past to God's mercy, the present to God's love and the future to God's providence."

—St. Augustine

O taste and see that the Lord [our God] is good! Blessed (happy, fortunate, to be envied) is the man who trusts and takes refuge in Him.

—*Psalm 34:8*

One of the biggest mistakes we make in relationships is when we try to make people be what we think they ought to be. Often we try to get them to be and think like us, but when we do that, we fail to realize God creates all of us very differently.

Ever notice how many of us are drawn to someone who is the opposite of us for a marriage partner or even a friend? Why is that? Because that person has what we are missing and we are attracted to it without even realizing it. This can be absolutely wonderful until we forget what attracted us to them in the beginning and we begin trying to change them to be more like us. Only God can change people and even He cannot change people if they are not willing to change.

Instead of "working on people," we should pray for them that they would be open to change and allow God to work in their lives. When we pray for others to change, we need to do so with a lot of humility, still keeping in mind we have faults of our own.

I can remember when Dave and I stood in a room and shook hands, making a commitment to accept and love each other "as is," faults and all. We had both been so busy trying to change the other, but the result was that neither of us was enjoying being together. From that day forward, things got better. We have to renew our commitment quite often, because it is easy to "fall off the wagon" and start trying to control again. But we do know without a doubt it is not our job to change each other. If you want to simplify your life, pray for the people in your life and let God be God!

48

Have a Broad Circle
of Inclusion

"The only gift is a portion of thyself."

—RALPH WALDO EMERSON

Above all things have intense and unfailing love for one another, for love covers a multitude of sins [forgives and disregards the offenses of others].

—1 Peter 4:8

God has called us to love everyone just as He loves us. God doesn't reject anyone, and we shouldn't either. The world is filled with lonely people who are perhaps a bit different or not easy to understand. Instead of avoiding those people, we should make every effort to reach out to them. There's a reason why each of us are the way we are; we need to remember that except for the grace of God in our lives, the people we reject could very well be ourselves. We need to keep our circles of friends broad and inclusive; at the minimum, we should avoid being exclusive to only those we feel are most like us.

I recall feeling very rejected much of my life. I could sense people did not like me and I really did not understand why. People would say to me, "Why do you act the way you do?" I could not give an answer because I didn't understand what it was about me that bothered them. I was just being the only me I knew how to be. I was sexually abused by my father and my personality became harsh and hard. I presented myself in a way that made people not like me and I acted like I didn't care. But the truth was, deep inside, I was desperate for love and acceptance.

It was only when Jesus accepted me unconditionally that I began to heal. Perhaps along with going to church, we should make an effort to *be* the church and actually do the work Jesus did. He had a broad circle of inclusion, and I find that to be much simpler than trying to decide if a person fits all the qualifications to be "in" my group. Perhaps if we stopped examining one another for flaws and just walked in love, we could all enjoy life much more.

49

Give It to God

"All that I have seen teaches me to trust God for all I have not seen."

—ANONYMOUS

Casting the whole of your care [all your anxieties, all your worries, all your concerns, once and for all] on Him, for He cares for you affectionately and cares about you watchfully.

—1 Peter 5:7

There has probably been a time in your life when you had a problem and someone said, "Just give it to God." Although that may not be the answer we want to hear at the time we are hurting, it is still the answer. A great deal of our unhappiness and confusion is a result of us trying to do what only God can do.

"Let go and let God be God" really is a good idea. It immediately simplifies any situation no matter how difficult. We need to do what we can and then cast the rest, along with our cares, on God. The Bible says we should do what the crisis requires and "having done all . . . , to stand" (Ephesians 6:13). The word "stand" translated in the original Greek means "to abide or rest in God." Life is not complicated when we are doing something that comes easy to us, but it can get downright overwhelming when we try to do what we know we cannot. Do your best and then let God do the rest!

Ask yourself if you are trying to be superhuman and do something that only God can do. If so, stop right now and give it to God. Say out loud, "This is something I cannot make happen and I release it to God right now." Now, feel the weight of it leave you and refuse to take it back. Even if God takes longer than you planned, do not take it back. Remember, all that burden did was make you miserable and the same thing will happen again if you keep welcoming it back with open arms. Keep life simple by, once and for all, casting all your cares on God, all your anxieties, all your worries, and all your concerns. Remember, it's because He cares for you (see 1 Peter 5:7)!

50

Take Control of Your Thoughts

"Drag your thoughts away from your troubles . . . by the
ears, by the heels, or any other way you can manage it."

—MARK TWAIN

Collect your thoughts, yes, unbend yourselves.

—*Zephaniah 2:1*

Confused and complicated thoughts produce a
confused and complicated approach to everything.
Where the mind goes, the man follows! If you want
your life to change, your thoughts must also change.
The Bible says in order to experience the good plan
God has for us, we must completely renew our minds.
We must learn to think like God thinks! Would God
worry about what you worry about? Would He think
the same things about people you have thought? The
truth is, it is not our circumstances making us so
unhappy; it is the way we look at them. As I said in
the beginning of this book, life is probably not going
to change, so we must change our approach to it.

You can begin a revolution in your life today by
simply changing the way you see things and think
about them. Can we control our thoughts, or do

we have to just think whatever comes to mind? Of course, we can control our thoughts. We have free will and can learn to choose our thoughts carefully. The mind is the battlefield, and Satan will certainly try to plant all kinds of wrong thoughts in our minds. He hopes we will receive his lies and that he will win the battle for our lives. You see, he knows if he gets our minds, he will get us.

God's Word teaches us to cast down wrong thoughts (see 2 Corinthians 10:4–5), and if God tells us to do it, then we can do it. Learn God's Word so you can know truth and be able to refuse to think on anything that enters your mind other than truth. I will admit it is a battle at first, but like any other battle, if you keep at it, you will win. You will experience victory!

You live in a house made of thoughts, so if it is time to remodel, get started right away. There is no time like the present to start thinking about things that will benefit you.

51 Don't Be Complicated

"Our life is frittered away by detail . . . simplify, simplify."

—Henry David Thoreau

The Lord preserves the simple; I was brought low, and He helped and saved me.

—*Psalm 116:6*

Since this book is about simplifying life, it might seem obvious that we should avoid being complicated, but just in case anyone is missing it, I thought I would talk about it. Are you like I once was? Can you complicate what begins as a simple gathering? Are you so addicted to trying to make things so perfect and impressive that they turn into a nightmare rather than the dream you had in mind?

Did you know most of the little details we struggle over are the ones nobody notices but us, and those numerous details are what keep us from enjoying the simple life? And, it turns out, the people we are trying to impress don't really care anyway.

When we built our first home, I remember laboring extensively over the water faucets and door handles. One day a friend asked me about my water faucets because she was now building a home, and

I could not even remember what my faucets looked like. Now that is sad! I frustrated myself over something I could not even visualize later. We have built two other homes since then, and I have yet to have anyone come into my home and stare at the water faucets and door knobs. If they are really important to you, spend all the time you want, but if in the long run it is not going to make that much difference, get something that looks good and move on.

Sometimes checking out all your options only confuses you. Most people (especially women) want to look at everything in town before making a decision, and more than likely they end up getting something they saw three days and fourteen stores ago they really liked but were too afraid to settle on. Or they get so confused, they end up getting nothing. If you want to simplify your life and save some time, try buying what you like when you see it and don't keep looking for days, just in case you see something you like better. Yes, occasionally you might see something and think, *Oh gee, I wish I would have seen that before I bought what I did*, but that rarely happens.

Work at having a simple approach to everything you do. Life is too short to live it frustrated.

52

Don't Plan for Perfection

"All of us occasionally do what is right. A few predomin-
antely do what is right. But do any of us always do what is
right?"

—Max Lucado

Let this same attitude and *purpose* and *[humble] mind be in
you which was in Christ Jesus: [Let Him be your example in
humility:].*

—*Philippians 2:5*

Unrealistic expectations can quickly steal your peace
and joy. We usually visualize a perfect day, with perfect people, and we are perfectly happy in our perfect
little world, but we all know that isn't reality. What is
real is that only God is perfect and the rest of us are
under construction.

The devil is alive and well on planet Earth and
he works relentlessly to mess up anything he can. He
knows what steals our peace and he sets us up to get
upset. Instead of freaking out when things don't go
exactly the way you planned, why not plan for some
"boo-boos"? In the last three days, I have broken a
dish (that was new), spilled water out of the humidi-
fier all over the floor, dropped the container of dog
food and worked at trying to keep my dog out of it

while I picked it up, and had four keys made for a door and found when I tried to use them that none of them worked—those are just the things that come to mind right away! I could probably think of more if I thought on it long enough.

These are the kinds of things that once got me very upset. I would huff and puff and murmur and complain and talk about how nothing ever worked out right. None of that stopped "boo-boos" from happening. As a matter of fact, my frustration caused me to lose my focus and create more accidents and mishaps. After years of letting the devil steal my peace—and I am quite sure laugh at me—while he watched me have my little fits, I finally got it! Life is not perfect and things are going to happen we did not plan for and would rather not have. My new attitude is, "Oh well, that's life!" I have discovered if I don't let those things impress me, then they can't depress me.

Everyone has to deal with inconveniences, but a person who is not childish can deal with them and avoid the bad attitude. This new attitude has greatly simplified my life. Now I don't have to get upset so much every day just because everything did not go my way. You don't either.

53

Be Easy to Get Along With

"Coming together is a beginning. Keeping together is progress. Working together is success."

—Henry Ford

Be of the same [agreeable] mind one with another; live in peace, and [then] the God of love [Who is the Source of affection, goodwill, love, and benevolence toward men] and the Author and Promoter of peace will be with you.

—2 Corinthians 13:11, emphasis added

Most of us probably wish people, in general, were easier to get along with, but have we considered how we ourselves score in that area? For example, how do you respond when you don't get your way? Do you get your feelings hurt easily? Are you insecure and need a lot of attention to feel good about yourself? How do you handle correction? Are you adaptable? Do you have very specific ways you want things done, and if they are not done that way, do you let everyone know you are not happy? There was a time in my life when my answer to all of those questions would have been embarrassing.

I wanted everyone else to change so I could be happy, but God showed me in many instances, I was the problem. The simple truth was that I was hard to please and easy to offend. I wanted my way and did not act very nice when I didn't get it. Of course, my attitude complicated my life because I spent a lot of time being upset. It is impossible to enjoy a simple life unless you're easy to get along with.

It was really difficult for me to admit in the beginning that I was hard to get along with, but once I did, it was the beginning of a whole new world for me. I quickly found it really was easier to adapt sometimes than to demand my own way and go through all the arguments to get it. I found if people did their best, I could compliment them instead of finding the one thing they did not do according to my specifications and making sure I corrected them about it. I learned that many things could just be let go, and it really would not make any difference in the overall outcome. With each of those petty things I was able to give up, my life was made one step simpler.

I am certainly not assuming all my readers are hard to get along with, but perhaps a few are. If you happen to be one of them, then I know how you feel, but I can assure you God will help you change if you are willing. You should start by admitting the truth, perhaps of all the ways you have been hard to get along with. Remember, only the truth will make you free (see John 8:32).

54 Don't Overestimate Yourself

"It was pride that changed angels into devils; it is humility that makes men as angels."

—Saint Augustine

A man's pride will bring him low, but he who is of a humble spirit will obtain honor.

—Proverbs 29:23

There's nothing wrong with believing in yourself. I believe it's important to have a good opinion of yourself because I don't think Jesus died for us so we could belittle and devalue ourselves. However, the Bible does teach us not to think more highly of ourselves than we ought to, but to judge our abilities soberly, remembering the grace of God (see Romans 12:3).

If we think too highly of ourselves, we will always end up thinking too little of others. Whatever we do well, we must remember God gave us the ability to do it. We should thank Him and never think less of someone else because their abilities are different than ours.

I like to think of myself as what I call an "everything-nothing": everything in Christ and nothing in myself, or as the Bible says, "I can do all things through

Christ" (see Philippians 4:13) and "Apart from Him I can do nothing" (see John 15:5).

Having a humble view of ourselves and being willing to serve others whose talents may not be as obvious is the simple approach to life. Jesus certainly lived a simple, enjoyable life and yet, His entire focus was on serving His heavenly Father as well as those He came into contact with each day.

A proud person ends up struggling a lot in relationships. They are judgmental and can easily find fault with others. They are not likely to succeed for long, because as the writer of Proverbs tells us, pride comes before destruction and a haughty spirit before a fall (see Proverbs 16:18).

When we have a proper attitude toward ourselves, it is the beginning of enjoying peace of mind. When we have peace of mind, we can truly begin to enjoy life.

55

Get Rid of Junk Mail

"Pity your poor mail carriers. Their shoulders must burn under the mailbag strap as they haul each day's mail to your desk."

—KEVIN A. MILLER

Avoid it . . . turn from it and pass on.

—*Proverbs 4:15*

Most of us get all kinds of mail we do not want. I can remember feeling somewhat guilty trying to throw mail away without reading it, until God showed me I am not obligated to read something just because somebody sent it to me uninvited. If I do that, then they are the ones controlling my life instead of me.

Have you ever purchased something by mail order only to find out three months later you were getting a hundred different magazines you never asked for? Then, did you call all of them and ask to be removed from their mailing list, never to be taken off? That's happened to me and I don't like it.

It is sad that today we can look at a pile of mail and feel overwhelmed before we even start going through it. I don't imagine we can keep people from sending it in today's society, but at least we don't have to keep it. Throw away mail you don't want. Don't keep it in case you ever get around to reading it. If it is not important enough to look at now, or at least in the next few days, chances are you will never look at it.

I have been as many as twenty issues behind in reading one little magazine I get. I kept piling them up, planning to read them someday. Then one day I got tired of looking at the pile and gave all of them away at the office. I still get one every month because someone sends it to me as a gift and I do enjoy it when time permits, but now I give it away when it comes in unless I know I will have time to read it soon.

The only way to avoid having piles of stuff all over the house, which is one of my biggest pet peeves, is to systematically move them on. Either throw them away or give them away if they have value, but for goodness' sake, don't just keep them!

56 Block Solicitors' Phone Calls

"I suppose some degree of commerce would grind to a halt if telephone solicitors weren't able to call people at home during dinner hour."

—Anonymous

And he is drawn in diverging directions [his interests are divided and he is distracted from his devotion to God].

—1 Corinthians 7:34

Do you get tired of answering the phone and talking to a computer that is trying to take a survey? How about an insurance salesman during dinner, or a credit card company trying to give you yet another credit card you don't need and should not want?

The good news is you can have all those calls blocked. You don't have to receive calls from solicitors. We had all of those calls blocked for years and then moved to a new house. We started getting calls all throughout the evening from insurance companies, loan companies, satellite companies—if they were selling something, they were calling us. At first, I could not figure out what was going on, and then I realized we had changed phone numbers and forgot to have the solicitor calls blocked.

One of the easiest ways to block unwanted telemarketers is to register your name and phone number on the National Do Not Call Registry (www. donotcall.gov). You can register as many phone numbers as you like, so don't forget to include your cell phones and office phones in addition to your home.

I am not against people who work as solicitors. I know they have to make a living like everyone else, but my life is too full already to take their calls. When I finally sit down in the evening, I don't want to jump up three or four times to talk to a computer or someone trying to sell me something I don't want. This might be one way you can increase your peace and save some time (as well as your sanity).

57

Don't Let Work Pile Up

"Idleness is a constant sin, and labor is a duty. Idleness is the devil's home for temptation and for unprofitable distracting musings; while labor profiteth others and ourselves."

—ANNE BAXTER

In everything I have pointed out to you [by example] that, by working diligently in this manner, we ought to assist the weak, being mindful of the words of the Lord Jesus, how He Himself said, It is more blessed (makes one happier and more to be envied) to give than to receive.

—*Acts 20:35*

Do you feel overwhelmed when you look around and seriously consider how many things you need to do? A good way to simplify your life is to never let work pile up. When you're facing a project you don't want to do, it is easy to decide to do it later, or wait until tomorrow. But you have to exercise willpower to stay with a task and not waste your time finding excuses to not finish your work. You may have heard the phrase "An idle brain is the devil's playground."

When we allow ourselves to be idle we can find a million excuses to keep us from getting busy. You may tell yourself, "I need more time to tackle that project than is available today"; or you may say, "I'm just too tired." You might simply convince yourself, "I'm just not capable of that right now." Whatever excuses you create, the truth is, if you were busy working, your mind wouldn't have time to come up with excuses and the work wouldn't pile up.

Living a simple life requires self-control. You must decide what needs to be done and systematically do it. No excuses! It may be tough at first, especially if you haven't been disciplined in the past, but the rewards of order and restraint are worth the effort. The Bible says that discipline brings peaceable fruit (see Hebrews 12:11).

If you believe in your heart that the project in question is something you are supposed to do then I encourage you to make a decision not to put it off unless you are faced with an emergency you cannot control. Set your mind and keep it set on getting the job done! When you do, you will feel better about yourself and you will have the simple joy of knowing that you did what was right.

58

Plan Ahead

"First say to yourself what you would be; and then do what you have to do."

—Epictetus

A man's mind plans his way, but the Lord directs his steps and makes them sure.

—*Proverbs 16:9*

I recently had an appointment with a nutritionist and personal trainer who is working with me so I can have optimum health and energy. After evaluating me and giving me my program he said, "It will be impossible for you to do this if you don't plan ahead." I have to intentionally plan to go to the whole foods store so I can have plenty of the right kinds of things in the house to eat. It is easy to make wrong food choices if you don't have healthy options available. When I travel, I have to plan ahead and take nonperishable food items with me that fit my program. When I eat out, I need to know what type of food the restaurant serves so I can make sure they have items on their menu meeting my requirements. All of these things take extra time and effort, but they are vital if I am going to end up with the result I desire.

I also have to really plan ahead in order to carve

out time to work out. I have to take weights and look for an opportunity to go to a gym. I have to get up early and possibly say no to other outings that will prevent me from fulfilling my goal. I don't have to be legalistic, but I do have to be disciplined.

Most of my life, I hated the idea of exercise programs and I was sure I did not have time for one until God actually showed me if I didn't get stronger, it would prevent me from fulfilling His calling on my life. It is amazing what we can do if we really want to. Most of the time we use the "I just didn't have time to" excuse for things we don't want to do. But the truth is we never take the time to do them. We all have the same amount of time every day, and what we do with it is up to us. At the very least, we should be honest with ourselves and others and say, "I don't do it because I don't want to put the time, energy, and effort into it." Truth is what frees us (see John 8:32) so if we get truthful, if we will get very honest with ourselves, perhaps we will see positive change.

These principles will help you in any area of your life, so I encourage you to prayerfully decide what you want to do with your time and then plan ahead so you actually end up doing it. If you really want to do something, you will have to be very determined not to let other things steal your time. You will have to order your life instead of letting it order you.

59

Buy Some Time

"Surround yourself with the best people you can find, delegate authority, and don't interfere as long as the policy you've decided upon is being carried out."

—RONALD REAGAN

To everything there is a season, and a time for every matter or purpose under heaven.

—*Ecclesiastes 3:1*

Does time feel shorter and shorter to you, even when you make the effort to plan ahead? If a shortage of time is your problem, then you might consider buying some. I don't mean you can get more than a twenty-four-hour day from the shopping mall, but you can buy yourself some time to do what you need to do by paying someone else to do some of the things that have to be done but don't necessarily have to be done by you.

If you can afford it, think about hiring someone to do housekeeping or laundry once a week or even once a month if that is what you can budget. Do you spend hours each month taking care of your yard, especially in the summer? You could consider paying a young boy or girl to pull weeds and save a few hours. They are usually anxious to make a few dollars, and if you overwork and have long-term stress you may end up spending the money on medicine or doctor bills anyway. Most of us immediately think we cannot afford to pay people to help us, but is that really true, or do we merely resist new thinking in these areas?

Some people have even said to me, "I should be able to get this done" or, "I just wouldn't feel right spending money on help." Perhaps you should ask yourself, why not? Some people just refuse to spend the money, so adamant about it they are willing to let their health or their family suffer for it. I believe we should be frugal, but not cheap. We may have to spend some money in order to make more money. We may have to seek help in some areas so we can thrive in the areas God wants.

People often desire to do new and exciting things, but they get stuck in an old way of thinking that prevents progress. We may think about all the things in life we want to do and even feel we are supposed to do, but instead, we get frustrated because we do not have the time. Those things may never get done unless we swallow our pride and buy some time.

I once did a lot of tasks I now pay someone else to do. If I didn't, I wouldn't even be writing this book right now because I would not have the time. If you need to simplify, this may be the answer you have been looking for. Buy some time and buy your life back.

Organize

"Don't agonize. Organize."

—FLORYNCE KENNEDY

She looks well to how things go in her household, and the bread of idleness (gossip, discontent, and self-pity) she will not eat.

—*Proverbs 31:27*

When my surroundings are organized, I feel organized. Likewise, when they are disorganized and cluttered, I feel the same way. My life feels very complicated if I don't keep my schedule organized as well as my home, clothes closet, work space, and . . . the list can keep going. In an effort to simplify my life and relieve stress, I decided I needed to be more organized, especially in the mornings. Getting out of the house on time in the mornings has been quite a challenge and if I do manage to leave on time, I am usually rushing, making me feel hot, irritable, and definitely not in a positive mood for starting the day! I finally decided a while back I would take some time the night before and pick out my clothes for the next day including shoes, purse, and jewelry. I now make a list of what I need to leave the house with and get as much of it together ahead of time as possible.

Joyce Meyer

By doing these things in the evening when I do have time, my mornings are simpler and more relaxed. Starting the day all stressed out is not a good choice. If we begin that way, sometimes it can stay like that all day. We have kicked everything off in high gear to get going, and it seems virtually impossible to shift to a slower gear once that happens.

Recently I was leaving on a three-week trip, which requires a lot of getting ready; and with this particular trip, we were on a shorter timeline than usual so it was even more vital for me to be really organized. We had two people coming at 6:00 a.m. the next morning to help us get everything loaded and to the airport. I had a lot of last-minute instructions to give them so I decided I would call each of them the night before and give them their list of duties so I did not have to deal with all those details in addition to getting ready myself the next morning. As it happened, one of them overslept and was late, but because I had covered so many of the details the previous evening we still got out on time and without feeling stressed. I also spent plenty of time getting all of my personal items packed throughout the week instead of rushing around at the last minute. Because I planned ahead, I was able to stay organized and it was a much different result than it could have been.

Some people say, "I'm just not organized." But I think anyone can be if they get a plan and discipline themselves to stick to it. Not leaving everything to the last minute is one of the first rules of being organized, so I suggest you start there and grow. You'll be amazed at how much you can accomplish and how good you'll feel doing it.

Keep Prayer Simple

"Do not pray for easy lives. Pray to be stronger men! Do not pray for tasks equal to your powers. Pray for power equal to your tasks."

—PHILLIP BROOKS

Let Your ear now be attentive and Your eyes open to listen to the prayer of Your servant which I pray before You day and night.

—*Nehemiah 1:6*

A lot of people struggle with their prayer life. They feel frustrated and confused, and I believe it is because we think that simple prayer can't be acceptable to God. Somehow we have bought into the idea that prayer must be eloquent, long, and perfect. God has challenged me to pray simply, telling Him what I want or need in the fewest words possible, yet being very sincere. I think we often try to say so much we lose our focus. We end up just rambling on and on and find it difficult to release our faith. We make it more about our words and less about Him.

One might pray for a long time but somehow feel they are not finished or as if their prayers did not get through to God. I also attribute this to not keeping prayer simple. For example, if you have sinned by not being truthful about something, you can try simply saying, "Father, I ask You to forgive me for being untruthful and I receive Your forgiveness now, In Jesus' name, amen!" Wait a few moments in God's Presence and receive by faith what you have just asked for. Now, if you need to make restitution by correcting your former statement to another person, go ahead and do that, but also realize you are no longer under condemnation. God has forgiven you so you can forgive yourself. Wow! That is simple, isn't it? Pray like this and you will feel your prayer is finished!

The entire nature of faith is simple. There is nothing complicated about it. Faith simply leans on, relies on, and trusts in God. Faith believes the Word of God. Faith knows God is faithful, and that nothing is impossible with Him.

God Himself is simple. When asked by Moses to explain who He was, God said, "I AM" (Exodus 3:14). When we search the Bible for the answer to all of our problems, we find it always says in simple, certain terms—"Believe" (see John 11:40). We are instructed to simply come to Him as a little child (see Luke 18:17). I don't find too many little children trying to be eloquent or impressive when asking their parents for something. They are plain, simple, and straightforward. Simple prayer will help produce a simple life, so get started right away praying prayers that God will listen to.

Live with Margin

"Half our life is spent trying to find something to do with the time we have rushed through life trying to save."

—Will Rogers

For David said, The Lord, the God of Israel has given peace and rest to His people.

—1 Chronicles 23:25

If you are like me, you don't like to waste one moment of time. You'd rather balance your checkbook while you're waiting in the doctor's office than read a magazine. You often make appointments and follow-up calls while you're sitting at the mechanic's or in the car line at your child's school. You pride yourself on never wasting time. That may sound right, but it isn't very realistic. When I plan everything too close in an effort not to waste any time, I always end up frustrated and rushing around trying not to be late. What we need is margin between things. That means we add time to each task or appointment we hope we won't need, but we make available just in case. I can finally acknowledge that absolutely everything takes a little longer than we think it will. Things we did not foresee like a last-minute phone call, car keys that cannot be located, or a cell phone forgotten can slow us down and complicate things greatly if we try to pack too much into the schedule. I frequently have times when I get into my car to drive away and have to go back into the house as many as three times to get things I forgot due to my rushing to get out.

It seems as though I have tried my entire life to avoid getting anywhere early with nothing to do but wait. I should also add that, until recently, I planned things without leaving margin and usually ended up either being late or getting there on time frustrated and stressed. But the good news is I am changing. I saw the light and now consistently plan extra time for the unexpected things I do not expect but almost always happen. I have not arrived yet, but I am determined to press on because I refuse to live a complicated life any longer.

It is better to do less with peace than it is to do more with stress. In what areas of your own life do you need to add margin? I suggest you start adding fifteen minutes to each item on your daily to-do list. You will probably end up using it, but if by chance you have some free time, try resting. Have a mini-vacation. Close your eyes, lay your head back, and relax. It will help prepare you for what's next on your schedule.

Joyce Meyer

63

Don't Have a False Sense of Responsibility

"We are all something, but none of us are everything."

—Blaise Pascal

My defense and *shield depend on God, Who saves the upright in heart.*

— *Psalm 7:10*

I have always been a very responsible person, so irresponsible people tend to irritate me. In the past, I frequently resented being responsible for what irresponsible people did not do, until God helped me realize I actually had a false sense of responsibility. A lot of what I did was not necessary. Perhaps some of you have the same dilemma.

Do you automatically step up to the plate and do whatever needs to be done, and then feel sorry for yourself because you have to do everything? You can be forever frustrated or you can make a decision to change. You may have been hurt or disappointed by someone who ignored their responsibility and now feel the only way to avoid more pain is to just do everything yourself. However, experience has taught me such reasoning only amplifies the problem. You may even be feeding irresponsibility in someone else by doing what they desperately need to learn to do themselves.

Far too often people don't do what they should, and then when they are in trouble they expect someone else to pay the price to get them out of it. When we love people, we want to help them, but there are times when tough love helps them more than emotional love. Just doing someone else's job feeds a lazy, immature, irresponsible attitude. Why not try letting them know that if they don't take care of business, they will pay the price, not you. Make sure you stick to your word.

I find if someone I depend on forgets something a couple of times then it's natural for me to just do it myself. It takes less time than making sure they do it. But what I have learned to do is make them take their responsibility and if they won't, I have to get someone who will. I don't like to hurt people, which is a good quality, but it can also become a problem if not kept in balance. We are not wise if we destroy our own lives trying to fix everyone else's.

I have often had a tendency to do things myself to make sure they are done the way I wanted. God taught me that a humble person realizes their way is not the only way and that allowing others to do things their way gives them room to be themselves. Your spouse doesn't put dishes away the same way as you, but the dishes still get put away. As long as the job gets done, does it really matter if it is done differently than you would do it?

If you find your life is complicated, try simplifying it by always doing your responsibility, but never doing someone else's unless it's an emergency. Start today and take an honest look at whether or not you really *have* to do all the things you are doing!

64

Don't Try to Take Care of Everybody

"I was so good at caretaking that I once found a piece of petrified wood and spent the next year trying to make it not be so afraid."

—TERRY KELLOGG

But let every person carefully scrutinize and examine and test his own conduct and his own work.

—*Galatians 6:4*

Are you a caretaker? Some people actually get their worth and value from taking care of everyone else. It becomes their identity and they are proud of it. However, most of them ultimately become martyrs. They take care of everyone and constantly complain about having to do it. They sacrifice themselves and make everyone feel guilty because they do.

The interesting thing about these types of people is you cannot keep them from doing what they do. They don't want help or an answer; they want to complain. I know a woman who talks about how she has sacrificed her entire life doing for others and how unfair it is, but she still latches on to anyone she can care for.

Some people, however, do feel they are in a trap

they want to get out of but simply don't know how. If that is you, I suggest you locate your true responsibility and give up the rest. Of course, there will be people who won't understand. They will get angry and may even say unkind things about you, but at least you may get a life and save your sanity.

I tried to help someone for four years who was a wounded individual reared in a very dysfunctional home. I wanted very much to see this individual have a chance at a good life. We spent time, money, and effort, and as long as we did everything for him, things moved in a good direction. Then the time came for him to get out on his own and take care of himself. He had a job, an apartment, a car, friends, and no reason not to succeed in life; however, as soon as we were no longer taking care of everything, he went back to all of his old ways. He would get into trouble and someone would call us to come get him. After the third time, we finally realized we wanted his healing and restoration more than he did and we had to let go.

If you have tried to help someone for years and they are still not "helped," you might want to consider whether or not they really want help. You may like to see change in their life, but maybe they don't want to change. If you want a simple life, then by all means help all the people you can, but don't become a professional caretaker who feels used up and burned out.

65

Give Up Control

"We may let go all things which we cannot carry into the eternal life."

—Anna R. Brown Lindsay

But you are not living the life of the flesh, you are living the life of the Spirit, if the [Holy] Spirit of God [really] dwells within you [directs and controls you]. But if anyone does not possess the [Holy] Spirit of Christ, he is none of His [he does not belong to Christ, is not truly a child of God].

—Romans 8:9

One of the books I've recently enjoyed reading is *Out of Control and Loving It* by Lisa Bevere. At first, it sounds like an odd title until you realize she means she no longer tries to control life and all the people in it; as a result, she enjoys her life more than ever.

I am a strong type A personality and come from a dysfunctional family where I was raised by a type A personality who was a master controller. As a result, by the time I reached adulthood, I also wanted to control everything and everybody. I still have to work on it at times and remind myself that everyone has a right to run their own life, but I have come a long way. I found life is anything but simple as long as we feel we need to control everything. God is in control and nobody else! Facing that fact and deciding to let go and let God be God is the pathway to simplicity.

In the evenings, I often want my husband, Dave, to watch a movie with me. He will agree but will occasionally ask me to wait for him to take a shower. Sometimes he gets caught up doing other things before the shower and soon an hour has gone by and Dave is still "getting ready to take a shower." By then, I am tired of waiting, and frustrated because he is moving too slow for my timetable. This has gone on for years and recently I thought, *Why do I care if Dave is on time to watch the movie or not?* I now say, "Babe, I am starting a movie at 7:00 p.m. if you want to watch it with me." I start the movie at the time I said and let him do what he wants to do without me trying to control him. I enjoy the evening, and he finally comes in and asks me all kinds of questions about what's happening. Now I am practicing not getting irritated about that. (Ha ha!)

There have also been times when Dave tells me he is going to turn on another television upstairs to just check the sports scores but will be down in fifteen minutes. The problem is that most of the time I never see him after that. It now makes me giggle when I realize how many evenings I got upset and nothing ever changed. Now I simply let him do what he wants to do. I may not have control of him, but I do control the remote control. (Halleleujah!)

66

Be Willing to Adapt

"Adapt yourself to the things among which your lot has been cast and love sincerely the fellow creatures with whom destiny has ordained that you shall live."

—Marcus Aurelius

And other seed [of the same kind] fell into good (well-adapted) soil and brought forth grain, growing up and increasing, and yielded up to thirty times as much, and sixty times as much, and even a hundred times as much as had been sown.

—Mark 4:8

If the song you sing is, "My way or no way," you are in for a rough life. Of course, there are mild-mannered people who let you have your way just to keep peace, but you may also run into some who won't do it your way, no matter what. By never learning to take your turn being the one who adapts and adjusts, you're much more likely to be angry or have someone angry at you. Your life certainly won't be simple.

A spirit of pride is at the root of unwillingness to adapt and adjust to the desires of others. God tells us in His Word if we will humble ourselves under His mighty hand, He will exalt us in due time (see 1 Peter 5:6). In other words, if we are willing to do whatever is necessary to accomplish the will of God, at the right time, God Himself will lift us to a place beyond anything we could ever do for ourselves.

Getting our own way is highly overrated. We struggle and argue to get what we want, but the truth is we are happier when we live to make others happy rather than catering to ourselves.

It is much simpler to adapt and hold your peace than it is to fight and war and end up in strife. Strife, or conflict, is a result of us trying to get the things we want instead of asking God for them and waiting for His right time (see James 4:1–2).

I struggled with this concept for years but finally decided peace was much more important than pride. I highly recommend that you be ready to adapt if you truly desire to simplify your life.

67

Don't Try to Change What You Cannot Change

"God give us grace to accept with serenity the things we cannot change . . ."

—REINHOLD NIEBUHR, "THE SERENITY PRAYER," PT. I

Do you know how God controls the clouds and makes his lightning flash . . . how the clouds hang poised, those wonders of him who is perfect in knowledge?

—*Job 37:15–16 niv*

Trying to do what you can't only produces frustration and feelings of failure. We must learn what we can do and what we aren't able to do. We are partners with God and, in a partnership, each party involved has a part. The partnership works best when each one does what they are good at.

I tried to change many things about me and around me that really only God could change. I tried to change my husband, my children, my neighbor, myself, and my circumstances. I kept failing, but I always had a new project I was "working" on. I said I was trusting God, but the truth was I trusted myself more. God's ways and timing are not the same as ours, so when we get tired of waiting, we usually take matters into our own hands. It does not cause

God to hurry and do what we want Him to do, but it actually ends up making our wait longer and more frustrating.

It is important to know what we can do and then do it, but it is equally important to know what we cannot do. Like the old saying says, "Don't spin your wheels and go nowhere." You can simplify your life by no longer trying to do what you can't. We do not have to be super-heroes. Give yourself permission to be who you are—an imperfect human being who needs help!

68

Change What You Can Change

"[God give us] . . . courage to change the things which should be changed . . ."

—Reinhold Neibuhr, "The Serenity Prayer," pt. 2

Remember that [by submission] you magnify God's work, of which men have sung.

—Job 36:24

Simplifying a complicated life only happens when it's the result of making positive changes, so we definitely need to change what we can change. Some people say they hate change, when really, they love the results of change; they just don't like the process.

When things change, we often feel disoriented for a period of time. We are not what we used to be and we are not sure yet what we will be. Anytime we step out boldly to make changes we take a chance that we might fail. What we change into may not be as good as what we have, but then again it could be much better. The only way to find out is to step out!

Have you thought about changing something for a long time and yet you have never actually taken steps to do it? Good intentions can become a deeper and deeper rut. God looks for those brave-hearted souls who hear His voice and act accordingly.

The only way you will ever discover what you *can* have is to give up what you *currently* have. Increase always demands investment. I had to leave a secure job at a church in order to start my own ministry. It was a frightening and lonely time for me, but deep down inside I knew I needed to make a change. I had to invest what I had, but I ended up with much more than I gave up.

Regularly making necessary changes will help keep life simple. As you prune (cut) things off that need to go, you de-clutter your life and make room for the fresh and new.

69

Be Realistic in Your Expectations

"Expect nothing, live frugally on surprise."

—ALICE WALKER

And now, Lord, what do I wait for and expect? My hope and expectation are in You.

—*Psalm 39:7*

If we expect something from someone we should really only expect from God, we will end up disappointed and frustrated. Ask God for what you want and need and trust Him to work through whoever He chooses. The Bible says Jesus knew human nature and therefore did not trust Himself to people (see John 2:24–25). He fully understood how imperfect people can be and how they are incapable of meeting all our expectations all of the time. He kept good relationships but at the same time was very realistic in His expectations.

I got hurt very badly several times in life by expecting people to give me what only God could give. One of the lessons I learned the hard way had to do with a sense of my own self-worth and value. For a long time, I looked to people to make me feel good about myself when, in reality, I had to find my true value in Jesus Christ and His love for me. If we place our hope and expectation in God, we will not be disappointed.

People usually don't intend to hurt us, but the truth is, we all hurt and disappoint one another simply because we have inherent weaknesses. We are naturally selfish and tend to do what is best for us instead of what is best for other people. As we mature spiritually through our relationship with Jesus, we can overcome these selfish tendencies, but while we are in the process of changing, we will make mistakes.

Sometimes we expect something from others who are not even aware of our expectations. We become hurt and angry because we feel let down, and the individual we are angry at may not even know what he or she did to hurt us. Make a decision to put your expectations in God. Trust *Him* for what you want and need and it will make life a lot simpler.

70

Progress Is Made One Step at a Time

"Patience and perseverance have a magical effect before which difficulties disappear and obstacles vanish."

—John Quincy Adams

But let endurance and *steadfastness* and *patience have full play* and *do a thorough work, so that you may be [people] perfectly and fully developed [with no defects], lacking in nothing.*

—James 1:4

Anything that grows and changes does so progressively. When a seed is planted in the ground, it does not immediately sprout and produce fruit. The farmer must be patient and so must we. God helps us defeat our enemies little by little (see Deuteronomy 7:22); rarely does He wipe them all out in one fell swoop. As we are diligent to study His Word, He changes us into His image, little by little (see 2 Corinthians 3:18). We inherit the promises of God through faith and patience (see Hebrews 10:36).

Being impatient only tends to make us miserable, and it does not make God hurry. His timing is perfect and the best thing we can do is make a decision to enjoy the journey. Enjoy every step of your progress, or you will waste a lot of your life being frustrated about something you cannot change.

Expecting instant gratification is an unrealistic expectation and will only leave you frustrated and disappointed. If you desire to simplify your life, then you must change the way you approach everything. Understanding that everything is a process which takes time will help you relax and enable you to enjoy every step of the way.

The fruit of patience is a seed resting in you, and as you wait with a good attitude, it develops and grows. You may not be where you want to be, but you are making progress!

71 Wise Up Before You Burn Out

> "We are made wise not by the recollection of our past, but by the responsibility for our future."
>
> —George Bernard Shaw

> *Happy (blessed, fortunate, enviable) is the man who finds skillful and godly Wisdom, and the man who gets understanding [drawing it forth from God's Word and life's experiences].*
>
> —*Proverbs 3:13*

Wisdom is realistic! Wise people acknowledge their limitations and avoid trying to be super human. God has no limitations and can do things through us we can never do on our own, but each of us can and will burn out if we don't use wisdom in our scheduling and the commitments we make.

Jesus said when we are weary and overburdened we should come to Him and He will give us rest (see Matthew 11:28). One of the ways He gives rest is by showing us what we need to change in our lives.

Have you ever suffered from burnout? I have and it's not fun; it's definitely not an experience I want to repeat. I love my ministry but I remember driving by our office complex one day and sticking my tongue out at it. At that moment, I thought, *I don't ever want to hear the name Joyce Meyer Ministries again.* Of course, I did not really mean that, but at that particular moment I thought I did. Why did I feel that way? I had just finished doing thirteen conferences in thirteen weekends and I was burned out. I needed a change of pace, some variety and rest. When I got it, I felt totally back to normal and ready to go again.

Burnout doesn't happen overnight. If you find yourself extra cranky, dragging into work and leaving early, caring less about what used to be really important, or feeling physically sick though there's not a clear diagnosis of what may be wrong with you, you may be experiencing symptoms of burnout. Some people ignore the warning signs and keep pushing until their burnout is so bad they never recover. They give up on things God truly intended them to do simply because they were not realistic about their own needs. The simple way to live is to pace yourself so you can accomplish a lot in life and not get derailed through burnout.

72 Cultivate Solitude

"I love people. I love my family, my children . . . but inside myself is a place where I live all alone and that's where you renew your springs that never dry up."

—PEARL S. BUCK

My people shall dwell in a peaceable habitation, in safe dwellings, and in quiet resting-places.

—Isaiah 32:18

Being alone and enjoying quiet time is very healing to our souls. Everyone needs regular time to reflect and allow the soul to quiet down. Your mind needs to rest; it needs to experience the peace found in solitude. Emotions need time to settle and level out. They need time to recover from daily life. When we feel weary and as if we cannot go on, solitude helps us find the determination we need to finish our course with joy.

Jesus regularly went off by Himself into the mountains to be alone. He was refreshed and strengthened through solitude. In the quiet, we hear from God, and we are reassured of the direction He wants us to take in life.

Without solitude, my life can get absolutely crazy. Nothing makes sense and I can feel overwhelmed by everyone's expectations. I don't know when to say yes and when to say no. My mind is confused, my emotions are on a rollercoaster, and I frequently want to run away. But after a little quiet time—some time, alone, in prayer and meditation—everything changes. I find wisdom and direction in the times of solitude.

I absolutely love solitude and the peace I find in those times. They prepare me for the rest of life. Make the effort to carve out time in your day, week, or even month to find some solitude. Get up extra early and watch the sun come up with God. Find a quiet spot at a park and enjoy the beauty of God's creation. Whatever you do, I urge you to cultivate solitude because it is truly where you find the answers to a simple life that can be enjoyed.

73 Be Eternally Minded

"Aim at heaven and you will get earth thrown in. Aim at earth and you get neither."

—C. S. LEWIS

And set your minds and *keep them set on what is above (the higher things), not on the things that are on the earth.*

—*Colossians 3:2*

So many people are only concerned with today or a few months down the road. At best, some are concerned with retirement. We think and plan in temporal terms, and God thinks and plans in eternal terms. We are more interested in what "feels good" right now, what produces immediate results. God has an eternal purpose planned for our lives.

One way to simplify our lives is to stop planning every aspect of our temporal lives and trust God as He guides us day by day. When we follow God He leads us to do not only what is best for right now, but also what is best for eternity. God sees and understands what we don't. He wants us to trust Him and His perfect timing.

If we keep our focus on the bigger—eternal—picture, we can eliminate a lot of the time we waste on worry over what isn't happening the way we believe it should. Wanting to know everything ahead of time is just our way of taking care of ourselves. Give up reasoning and enjoy the beautiful, simple, powerful life God has waiting for you; as well as the eternal blessings that come from trusting His will for our lives.

74 Tackle Each Day as It Comes

"Live neither in the past nor in the future, but let each day's work absorb your entire energies, and satisfy your widest ambition."

—Sir William Osler

Therefore I always exercise and *discipline myself [mortifying my body, deadening my carnal affections, bodily appetites, and worldly desires, endeavoring in all respects] to have a clear (unshaken, blameless) conscience, void of offense toward God and toward men.*

—Acts 24:16

Duties we ignore can pile up and soon feel overwhelming, but daily discipline keeps us in a place to handle life peaceably. God's Word states no discipline for the present seems joyous, but later on it yields the peaceable fruit of righteousness (see Hebrews 12:11). In other words, it may be a challenge and require discipline to do what is right now, but the knowledge we have done what we were supposed to do is what gives us peace.

A little daily discipline protects us from suddenly finding we have more to do than is humanly possible. If we put things off that need to be done now, that does not prevent them from needing to be done. It only adds today's duties to tomorrow; and day after day, things pile up and soon life is so confusing, frustrating, and overwhelming, we get depressed and discouraged.

Discipline means we must frequently say no to the fleshly desire to put things off that need to be done now. The apostle Paul said, "I die daily." He did not mean he daily experienced physical death, but he did say no to himself regularly if what he desired did not agree with what the Holy Spirit was leading him to do.

If your discipline muscles are weak from lack of use, I recommend you begin getting them in shape today. They may hurt and feel sore at first, but soon you will be enjoying a peaceful, simple life.

75

Remember That God
Is for You

"If our confidence in God had to depend upon our confidence in any human person, we would be on shifting sand."

—FRANCIS SCHAEFFER

God is faithful (reliable, trustworthy, and therefore ever true to His promise, and He can be depended on).

—*1 Corinthians 1:9*

Statistics prove that 10 percent of the people we encounter will not like us. There is nothing we can do about it, except worry, but even that won't change their minds.

The truth is, God is for us and since He is so mighty and awesome, it really does not matter all that much who is against us (see Romans 8:31). Think about who is on your side, not who is against you. There are many people who do love and accept you and it is much more enjoyable to keep your mind on them. We should practice meditating on what we do have, not what we are missing. We do have God. He promises never to leave us or forsake us, so we are never without Him. He is more than enough.

When you hear someone does not like you or is

unhappy with you, don't let this information upset you. Stay focused on Jesus; He's your best friend, anyway.

If you are facing a tremendous challenge right now, one you feel is too much for you, take a moment and say these words out loud: "God is for me, and since He is for me, I can do whatever I need to do in life."

The Holy Spirit walks alongside us. He is the Standby, the Helper we can always rely on in life. You are never alone!

76

You Are More than a Conqueror

"Make me a captive, Lord, And then I shall be free. Force me to render up my sword, And I shall conqueror be."

—George Matheson

Yet amid all these things we are more than conquerors and *gain a surpassing victory through Him Who loved us.*

—Romans 8:37

If we begin believing life is too much for us and adopt a "give-up" attitude, we make a big mistake and buy into a lie. The truth is, we are more than conquerors through Christ Who loves us (see Romans 8:37). To me, being more than a conqueror means I know when I begin a trial that I will have the victory. We don't have to worry or be afraid—God is on our side and we are more than conquerors. We may feel like David in the Bible, standing before Goliath with nothing more than a slingshot, but we have the assurance of God that He is standing with us.

There is nothing in creation—no problem too big that can separate us from the love of God found in Jesus—if we don't allow it. When you feel overwhelmed, say, "God loves me and I am more than a conqueror through Him." Don't believe the devil's lies when he tries to tell you that you are not going to make it this time. Stop right now and purposely recall other victories you have had in the past. There have been other times when you probably felt you couldn't go on and yet you are still here. That is a testimony in itself. You are an overcomer!

Be careful how you talk during difficulty because your words affect you. They can strengthen or weaken you depending on what kind of words they are. Be positive. Think victory. Believe God, working in you, is enabling you to do anything you must. This God-kind-of-attitude helps you enjoy life at all times.

Pray *Before* You Have an Emergency

"Prayer is as natural an expression of faith as breathing is of life."

—Jonathan Edwards

Let my prayer come before You and really enter into Your presence; incline Your ear to my cry!

—*Psalm 88:2*

The apostle Paul thanked God for giving him the needed strength to handle every situation in life. I believe he did so as a matter of habit, and not necessarily because he had an emergency. Praying ahead of time gets us the help we need even before we need it. It shows we depend on God and trust Him to take care of things we do not even know about yet.

The way we release our faith is through prayer. Don't wait until you need faith to try and develop it. It may be too late then. Develop and release your faith before you're in a situation that requires it. Each morning, I pray God will help me with the day. I don't even know yet what the day will bring. I have plans all the time, but things happen every day we have not planned, and I want to be ready for them and not taken by surprise. I ask God to release the angels that are assigned to me, to go ahead of me and prepare my way. "You have not because you ask not" (see James 4:2) so why wait until you have problems? Why not pray early and have the help you are going to need already waiting for you?

Praying before you have an emergency is like putting money in the bank. If you have money set aside, then a car problem you were not expecting does not need to upset you. You have provided a way to continue living a simple, joy-filled life *before* you experienced a need. Start today getting some prayers in reserve. Fill up your prayer tank and you will avoid constantly living in crisis mode.

78 Keep Your Conscience Clear

"If we put off repentance another day, we have a day
more to repent of, and a day less to repent in"

—Anonymous

*But if your eye is unsound, your whole body will be full of
darkness. If then the very light in you [your conscience] is
darkened, how dense is that darkness!*

—Matthew 6:23

We should, at all times, strive to have a conscience void of offense toward God and man. Nothing complicates life like a guilty conscience. It pressures us and prevents us from truly enjoying anything. We may try to ignore it, but it is always whispering to us and reminding us we have not done what is right.

There are only two ways to live with a clear conscience. The first is to do what is right; and if we fail in that, we move to the second choice, which is to be quick to repent, to admit our sins, and to ask for God's forgiveness—and man's if necessary. We should determine to do our best in life; it is only then we will feel better about everything. We may still fail, but at least we have the comfort of knowing we did not fail on purpose.

A guilty conscience hinders our faith and worship.

It actually puts a stumbling block between us and God until it is removed. When we sin against other people, we will feel guilty when we are with them until we resolve the situation by apologizing. Don't live with a guilty conscience. It puts a dark cloud over everything and you cannot truly enjoy life.

There is no harder pillow than a guilty conscience. We will toss and turn at night if our conscience is condemning us and we try to ignore it. Take some time to examine your heart. Are there people in your life to whom you aren't speaking? Are there others you have wronged? Are there misunderstandings or hard feelings you need to put to rest with a friend? Take an honest self-examination of yourself and work to remedy those broken relationships. Your conscience will thank you and God will be proud of you.

79 Understand Righteousness

"He who created you without you will not justify you without you."

—St. Augustine

The heavens declare His righteousness, and all the peoples see His glory.

—*Psalm 97:6*

Some people have an overactive conscience. They feel guilty as a matter of habit, and not necessarily because they have truly done something wrong. The way to overcome this problem is to study what the Bible has to say about righteousness. If you don't understand the God-kind of righteousness, then you will spend your life trying to earn your own righteousness through good works.

It is important to understand the difference in your "who" and your "do." My children may not always do what I want, but they never stop being my children and I never stop loving them. God is the same way, only better. God gives us right standing with Him when we receive Jesus as our Savior (see 2 Corinthians 5:21). He "imputes" it to us, or credits it to our account (see Romans 4:11). He views us as righteous, which is the only standing acceptable to God. It is the only way we can fellowship with Him, because light cannot fellowship with darkness.

Since God in His mercy has made us righteous, we can learn to manifest right behavior. It is a process that takes time, but gradually we improve in how we behave. Our "do" improves. However, while it is improving, it is vital for us to remember "who" we are in Christ. We are God's child; He loves us and understands us. We are no huge surprise to Him. He knew all about us when He invited us into relationship with Him.

Understanding the biblical doctrine of righteousness will greatly simplify your life because, without it, you will always feel bad about yourself for one reason or another. Guilty feelings are very complicated and not easy to live with. Put on the simple garment of righteousness and start really living the life Jesus purchased for you through His death and resurrection.

80 Grace, Grace, and More Grace

"Our worst days are never so bad that you are beyond the reach of God's grace. And your best days are never so good that you are beyond the need of God's grace."

—JERRY BRIDGES

But He gives us more and more grace (power of the Holy Spirit, to meet this evil tendency and all others fully). That is why He says, God sets Himself against the proud and haughty, but gives grace [continually] to the lowly (those who are humble enough to receive it).

—James 4:6

Grace is the power of the Holy Spirit offered to us free of charge, enabling us to do with ease what we could never do alone with any amount of struggle and effort. Scripture encourages us to receive not only grace but *more* grace. Where sin abounds, grace does much more abound (see Romans 5:20). God has enough grace to meet all our needs, but we need to ask for it and learn to live in it.

When we attempt works of the flesh, we use up our own energy trying to do what only God can do. Works of the flesh produce frustration and work in direct opposition to grace. We really cannot live with a little of each because they cancel each other out.

Each time I feel frustrated I remind myself I am not receiving grace (God's energy) for the task at hand.

Frustration, complication, and misery are available in abundance, but so is God's grace. We are to humble ourselves under His mighty hand because only the humble get help. God helps those who humble themselves and admit they cannot do what needs to be done without His help.

Grace meets our evil tendencies (see James 4:6). It is the only thing that can change us into what God desires us to be, and He desires us to be like Him. Your life can be greatly simplified by learning how to receive grace in every situation. Without it, we all labor with life and everything becomes hard, difficult, and usually impossible.

81

Bridle Your Tongue

"Men are born with two eyes, but only one tongue, in order that they should see twice as much as they say."

—Charles Caleb Colton

Keep your tongue from evil and your lips from speaking deceit.

—Psalm 34:13

Put a restraint on your tongue and stop going through life saying whatever you want to say whenever you want to say it. "If anyone thinks himself to be religious (piously observant of the external duties of his faith) and does not bridle his tongue but deludes his own heart, this person's religious service is worthless" (James 1:26).

Ponder that scripture and think about how many "religious" people there are in the world who do not bridle their tongue. They speak in negative terms all the time; they gossip, criticize, judge, murmur, complain, and curse. They go to church but use no discipline in what they say. The Bible makes it very clear their religious service is worthless.

A lot of our problems are rooted in our own words. The power of life and death is in the tongue, and we must be satisfied with the result of our words (see Proverbs 18:21). I urge you to be careful about what you say. Anyone who never offends in speech is a perfect man, able to control his whole body, curb his nature, and, I believe, affect his destiny (see James 3:2).

Are you dissatisfied with your life right now? Perhaps you have now what you have said in the past. Are you ready to offer your mouth to God to be used in His service? If you are, then I believe you are on the road to a better life.

82

The Battle Belongs to the Lord

"We shall not fight our battles alone. There is a just God who presides over the destinies of nations, and who will raise up friends to fight our battles for us."

—Patrick Henry

The Lord will fight for you, and you shall hold your peace and *remain at rest.*

—*Exodus 14:14*

Complication is often the result of not trusting God to fight our battles for us. The Israelites were between the Red Sea and the Egyptian army, which was a frightening place to be. They were crying and wanting to run away but God sent a message through Moses saying, "The Lord will fight for you and you shall hold your peace *and* remain at rest."

When three armies came against Jehoshaphat and the people, their first inclination was to be afraid. But they intentionally set themselves apart to seek God, and He told them, "Be not afraid or dismayed at this great multitude; for the battle is not yours, but God's" (2 Chronicles 20:15).

How do you see battles; are they yours or God's? Remember, it is not what happens in life that makes it so complicated, but it is the way we approach what happens that stirs up stress and strife. It is the mind-set we embrace which determines whether or not we experience peace or turmoil.

When Jehoshaphat began worshiping God, he sent singers out to sing and others were appointed to praise. Soon the armies became confused and slaughtered one another. Do you want to live in confusion, or would you rather confuse the enemy? Begin to worship, praise, and sing, and do it, especially, when you have a problem. God will fight your battles for you and you can continue enjoying your life while you wait for His victory.

Avoid Scenes of Temptation

"When you flee temptation, don't leave a forwarding address."

—Anonymous

All of you must keep awake (give strict attention, be cautious and active) and watch and pray, that you may not come into temptation. The spirit indeed is willing, but the flesh is weak.

—Matthew 26:41

I suppose all of us wish we were never tempted to do wrong things, but that is not reality. The Bible says temptation must come, but why? If we were never tempted to do wrong, we could never exercise our free will to do right. God does not want robots or puppets serving Him; He wants free people who choose to serve Him. He sets before us life and death and urges us to choose life (see Deuteronomy 30:19).

The moment you feel tempted to do wrong, say no and get away from the temptation. If you had a problem with alcohol in the past, don't go to the bars planning not to drink alcohol. If you had a problem with drugs and were delivered, don't spend the day with people who use drugs. If you tend to abuse sweets, don't keep cookies, candy, and cake in the house.

Sometimes we say we don't want to do something and we pray for God to deliver us, yet we continue making provision for that very thing which tempts us. Perhaps the truth is we really don't want to be free as much as we say we do. We must be honest with ourselves and realize the flesh is weak.

The apostle Paul said to "make no provision for [indulging] the flesh [put a stop to thinking about the evil cravings of your physical nature] to [gratify its] desires (lusts)" (Romans 13:14). Get it off your mind and out of your sight and you are more likely to avoid temptation.

84

Avoid People Who Talk Too Much

"Whoever gossips to you will gossip about you."

—SPANISH PROVERB

He who goes about as a talebearer reveals secrets; therefore associate not with him who talks too freely.

—*Proverbs 20:19*

People who talk too much usually have problems in which you are wise not to take part; therefore, avoiding these people helps simplify our lives.

When people have no discipline over their mouths, they usually lack discipline in other areas as well. It is best for us if we are in close relationship with people who will urge us to come up higher in our choices. Spending excessive time with, and opening your heart to, those who pull you down in life is not wise at all. Think about who your friends are and start really listening to them, because you can tell a lot about a person's character by listening to what they say. Avoid people who gossip. If they gossip about someone else to you, they will gossip about you too.

When people talk too freely, they often don't do what they said they would do simply because they did not count the cost before making the commitment. They will disappoint you over and over again. You will be frustrated, but you may be the only one who can simplify that area of your life by avoiding those people. I am not suggesting we be rude to anyone, but we cannot let people mess up our lives just to keep them from getting their feelings hurt.

One of the best things you can do is choose your friends wisely. Guard your heart with all diligence, for out of it flow the issues of life (see Proverbs 4:23). I have greatly simplified my life by making a few adjustments concerning the people with whom I spend my time.

85

Be Generous

"All my experience in the world teaches me that in ninety-nine cases out of a hundred, the safe and just side of a question is the generous and merciful side."

—ANNA JAMESON

There are those who [generously] scatter abroad, and yet increase more; there are those who withhold more than is fitting or what is justly due, but it results only in want. The liberal person shall be enriched, and he who waters shall himself be watered.

—*Proverbs 11:24–25*

One of the wisest things anyone can do is be generous. When we help other people, we really help ourselves even more. To experience the joy of giving is what I call real living. Greed steals life, but generosity releases it along with amazing joy. I spent many unhappy years being selfish and concerned about what I could get out of life. As I cried out to God, asking Him to show me what was wrong in my life, one of the things He taught me was how I needed to be more generous instead of stingy.

I encourage you to look for opportunities to be a blessing to others. Be aggressively generous! Don't just give when you feel you have to, but always do more than required. Go the extra mile as the Bible teaches.

I heard the story of a woman who was terribly depressed. She went to her pastor for counseling and he told her to go home and bake three batches of cookies and give them away that week and come back the following week for another appointment. The woman never returned, but one Sunday after church the pastor saw her and asked why she did not return for her appointment. She told him she got so happy when she started baking cookies and giving them away she got over her depression.

Depression can be caused by a number of things, but I believe one of them is being self-centered and stingy. Do all you can, as often as you can, for as many people as you can, and you will be much happier. Believe it or not, being generous is much simpler than being selfish.

86

Be Wise

"Knowledge comes, but wisdom lingers."

—Alfred Lord Tennyson

Hear instruction and be wise, and do not refuse or neglect it.

—*Proverbs 8:33*

The Bible says wisdom is pleasure and relaxation to a man of understanding (see Proverbs 10:23). Wisdom is choosing to do now what you will be happy with later on. For example, wisdom does not spend all of its money now, but it saves some for the future, knowing it is wise to do so. Wisdom doesn't put off today's work until tomorrow because it knows it will then have two days of work to do in one. Wisdom is not a procrastinator; it takes action.

If you want to simplify your life, you must think about the future and realize the choices you make today will affect tomorrow. Some people are never able to relax and enjoy life because every day they deal with messes resulting from not walking in wisdom. I frequently hear people say, "I know I shouldn't do this, but . . . !" It is foolish to do things we know we should not do when we do them. How can anyone expect to get a right result if they already know they are making a wrong decision? They are gambling on things turning out right anyway, but wisdom does not gamble, it invests. Doing the right things now may not bring pleasure right away, but it does later on. Some people pay a high price for a cheap thrill, but you can make a decision right now to not be one of them.

We possibly make a million decisions in our lifetime, and the wiser they are, the better our lives will be. Simplifying your life requires that you really think about your decisions before you make them. As you contemplate a decision you're making today, ask yourself if you truly believe you will be happy with the results of that decision later in life. If you can't say yes, then maybe it's time to rethink that decision.

87

Beware of Distractions

"By prevailing over all obstacles and distractions, one may unfailingly arrive at his chosen goal or destination."

—Christopher Columbus

Then the cares and anxieties of the world and distractions of the age, and the pleasure and delight and false glamour and deceitfulness of riches, and the craving and passionate desire for other things creep in and choke and suffocate the Word, and it becomes fruitless.

—*Mark 4:19*

We often look at the devil as the author of our destruction, but he is actually more the author of our distraction. If he can distract us from our God-given purpose, he can cause us to bear no good fruit in life. God is glorified when we bear good fruit so, obviously, the devil wants to do anything he can to prevent that.

It is easy to get distracted in life; it is not something we have to try to do. We do, however, need to really discipline ourselves in order not to get distracted. Each person has many demands and expectations placed on them. It seems every person in our life expects something, and quite often, we find it confusing to know when to say yes and when to say no. Our spouses, friends, parents, children, other relatives, employers, government, churches, and neighborhood all expect us to do different things. It can be overwhelming and tiring.

While trying to meet all of these expectations, we frequently find they distract us from our main goal, which is following the will of God. If you are a people pleaser, then you know it is not difficult at all for the devil to distract you. He can easily lead you to dissatisfied people, and cause you to spend your life trying to make them happy. I finally realized a lot of the people I was trying to keep happy had already decided they were not going to be happy no matter what anyone did. They were basically miserable, dissatisfied, unhappy, and being used by the devil to make me unhappy.

The Bible teaches us not to get entangled or distracted, but to focus on Jesus (see Hebrews 12:2). Remember, the more you focus on the truly important things in your life, the simpler life will be.

88 Don't Be Easily Offended

"His heart was like a sensitive plant, that opens for a moment in the sunshine, but curls up and shrinks into itself at the slightest touch of the finger, or the lightest breath of wind."

—ANNE BRONTË

Understand [this], my beloved brethren. Let every man be quick to hear [a ready listener], slow to speak, slow to take offense and to get angry.

—James 1:19

A wise person ignores an insult. I once heard a story about Kathryn Kuhlman, a woman with a very wonderful miracle ministry. Anyone in the public eye will inevitably deal with people who judge, criticize, and even say and publish things about them that are not true. This happened to Miss Kuhlman frequently, but she refused to get offended because she knew it would be harmful to her relationship with God. She also realized taking and holding on to offense would steal her joy and would not do her any good at all.

God promises to be our vindicator if we will do things His way, and His way is to forgive. People often asked Miss Kuhlman how she could be friendly with people who said such ugly things about her and she responded by saying, "Oh, we are just going to pretend that never happened."

Has someone hurt your feelings recently? Are you offended? Do you need to forgive someone?

If your answer to any of these questions is yes, then I highly recommend you do what the Bible says to do. Pray for your enemies, bless, and do not curse them. Make a decision to forgive and trust God to heal your wounded emotions. If you see the person who hurt you, do your best to be friendly and treat them the way you honestly believe God would. The quicker you forgive, the less likely you are to get a root of bitterness in your heart, and the simpler your life will be.

89 Don't Be So Hard on Yourself

"Lay down the bat, and pick up a feather."

—ANONYMOUS

*Take My yoke upon you and learn of Me, for I am gentle (meek)
and humble (lowly) in heart, and you will find rest (relief and
ease and refreshment and recreation and blessed quiet) for
your souls.*

—*Matthew 11:29*

Are you quick to judge and criticize yourself? If so, I highly recommend you read Matthew 11:28–30. Jesus said He is not harsh, hard, sharp, and pressing; but He is humble, gentle, meek, and lowly. If God is not hard on us, then we don't need to be so hard on ourselves. Do you need a second chance? God gave Jonah one, and He gave Peter one, so why wouldn't He be willing to give you one too?

Ask Him for a second chance or a third, fourth, fifth, or whatever you need. God is full of mercy and He is long-suffering. His loving-kindness never fails or comes to an end. If we keep an account of all our shortcomings and failures, we will feel oppressed. Jesus came to lift burdens, but we must be willing to believe He is greater than our mistakes. I don't believe God is nearly as hard to please as we often think. After all, we are no surprise to Him. He knew all about each of us before He ever invited us into relationship with Him. If your life seems complicated, then perhaps you are simply too hard on yourself. Give yourself a break. Perhaps, if you receive more mercy from God for yourself, you will be able to extend mercy to others also.

God sees your heart and is always willing to work with anyone who refuses to give up. Keep pressing on and remember to let go of what is in the past. That may be the past of ten years ago or even five minutes ago. The point is, if it is past then you have to let it go and press on.

90

It Is Never Too Late to Begin Again

"How wonderful it is that nobody need wait a single moment before starting to improve the world."

—ANNE FRANK

It is because of the Lord's mercy and *loving-kindness that we are not consumed, because His [tender] compassions fail not. They are new every morning; great* and *abundant is Your stability* and *faithfulness.*

—*Lamentations 3:22–23*

Hopelessness is a burden none of us needs to endure because, with God, it is never too late to begin again. He is the God of new beginnings. Jonah went in the opposite direction of the one God instructed, but God let him have a fresh start once he admitted his mistake.

It is never too late to pray and ask for God's help and forgiveness. The devil wants us to feel hopeless. He loves words like "never" and "the end." He says, "This is the end of everything. You have messed up and can never overcome your bad choices." We must remember to look to God's Word for truth, because the devil is a liar.

The Bible is filled with stories about people who

experienced new beginnings. Receiving Jesus as our Savior is the ultimate new beginning. We become new creatures with an opportunity to learn a new way of living. The Bible even says in Ephesians 4:23 that we must be constantly renewed in our minds and attitudes. If you ever thought or displayed an attitude thinking it was too late for you to have a good life, good relationships, or hope for the future, then you need to renew your mind right away. Choose to think according to God's Word and not how you feel. Nobody is a failure unless they choose to stop trying. Life gets a lot sweeter and easier if we live with the attitude that says, "I will do my best today and I trust God will do the rest. Tomorrow I will begin again and I will never quit or give up."

91 Become like a Little Child

"Faith is unutterable trust in God, trust which never dreams that He will not stand by us."

—OSWALD CHAMBERS

In peace I will both lie down and sleep, for You Lord, alone make me dwell in safety and *confident trust.*

—*Psalm 4:8*

If you want a simpler life, you must learn to develop a more trusting life. Far too often, we don't allow ourselves to trust. We don't trust our spouses, we don't trust our kids, and if we're honest, many times we don't really trust God to do what He says He will.

Children usually don't have this problem of distrust. That's why they climb and hang from the highest tree branches, run full steam down steep hills, and jump off high-diving boards into the waiting arms of their parents. They trust their parents to be there to catch them, or at least pick them up if they fall. That's the same kind of trust God wants from us.

The person who trusts God knows even if things don't go the way he hopes, God will have a better plan than he did anyway. God has the future all planned out, and He knows the answer to everything. His

Word promises us He will take care of us *if* we trust in Him (see Psalm 37:5).

When we don't allow ourselves to trust God, we allow fear and worry to come in and take up residence in our lives. However, by placing our trust in Him, we remove those doubts; we can look to God and trust in His faithfulness and be confident He will not let us down or disappoint us. If we don't actively give our trust to God, we will carry burdens we were never meant to bear alone.

Trusting God brings a supernatural rest into our souls, allowing us to live simply and freely, the way He wants us to live. Trust doesn't just appear in our lives, but grows as we take steps of faith and experience God's faithfulness. Ask God to help you develop a deep trust of Him so He can show you all He has planned for your life.

92

The Person Who Lives
Inside You

"Keep your heart pure. A pure heart is necessary to see
God in each other. If you see God in each other, there is
love for each other, then there is peace."

—Mother Teresa

Since by your obedience to the Truth through the [Holy]
Spirit *you have purified your hearts for the sincere affection
of the brethren, [see that you] love one another fervently from
a* pure *heart.*

—1 Peter 1:22

We all have someone living inside us. He is called
the hidden man of the heart, and if we are going to
enjoy life, we must like that person. The importance
of a right heart cannot be overestimated. God looks
on the heart of man; He despises an evil heart but
loves a righteous one. God delights in a person who
wants to do what is right even if he does not always
succeed. I believe God would rather have someone
with a right heart who makes mistakes, than someone who has a perfect performance but holds on to a
wicked heart.

God also delights in a peaceful heart, one not anxious or upset. Having peace in our hearts proves we

are truly trusting God in all matters pertaining to life that concern us. When our hearts lean one way inside of us, but we ignore that sign and pretend to feel another way or act in a way that's not true to who we really are, it makes life extremely complicated. We have to pretend in everything, which certainly keeps life from being simple. Have you ever heard the phrase "Pure and Simple"? I used to keep a sign on my desk with that statement on it because I wanted to remind myself—if I wanted a simple life, I had to keep a pure heart.

Get to know the hidden man of the heart. Do some soul-searching and ask yourself if what you show people is the real you or someone else you have invented. If you need a change then begin by asking God to purify your heart. Start by examining your thoughts and attitudes. Facing truth is not always easy, but it is the beginning of having a life really worth living.

93

Don't Be Discouraged
with Yourself

"Permanence, perseverance and persistence in spite of all obstacles, discouragement, and impossibilities: It is this, that in all things distinguishes the strong soul from the weak."

—Thomas Carlyle

Therefore we do not become discouraged (utterly spiritless, exhausted, and wearied out through fear). Though our outer man is [progressively] decaying and wasting away, yet our inner self is being [progressively] renewed day after day.

—2 Corinthians 4:16

Babies learn to walk by taking one step at a time, and while they learn, they frequently fall down. This process takes place over and over again until they finally learn to walk. If they became so discouraged they quit trying, they would never learn to walk. We may get discouraged, but when we do, we must remember everyone goes through the same types of things. These things are often designed to check our character and faith. Will we give up or will we get up and try again? The Bible says the righteous man falls seven times and rises again. You see, even righteous men fall. None of us manifests perfection while we are in fleshly bodies.

When God gives us instructions, He often only shows us one step to take. It's natural for us to want the entire blueprint, but that's not how God works. If we take that one step, then we are given another and another until we finally reach our destination. Many people refuse to take one until they think they have their entire future figured out; these are the people who usually end up as failures in life.

Even those willing to take these important steps one step at a time will make mistakes and have to try again. Those who get discouraged with themselves and quit somewhere along the way will live miserable, fruitless lives. But it doesn't have to be that way. If we say we trust God, we must trust Him all along the way. It is not about the destination as much as it is about the journey.

Discouragement is complicated because it comes with a load of other negative emotions. Faith, on the other hand, is very simple. We do what we can do and trust God to do what we cannot. This attitude leaves us free to enjoy life and is the attitude God wants us to live with.

94

Be a Prisoner of Hope

"Hope is the thing with feathers that perches in the soul, and sings the tune without the words, and never stops at all."

—Emily Dickenson

Return to the stronghold [of security and prosperity], you prisoners of hope; even today do I declare that I will restore double your former prosperity to you.

—Zechariah 9:12

The Bible mentions prisoners of hope (see Zechariah 9:12). What is that? I believe it is someone who absolutely refuses to stop hoping no matter how desperate his circumstances are. Prisoners of hope are swept up and locked in to hope; they just can't get away from it. They must hope in God and believe something good is going to happen.

I think Abraham must have been a prisoner of hope. The Bible tells us he had no human reason to hope, yet he hoped, in faith, that the promise of God would manifest in his life. Hope deferred makes the heart sick, and it causes depression, discouragement, and despair. When you have hope, you intentionally become positive in your thoughts and attitudes. Hope also talks positively. Hope believes all things are possible with God and it expects good news at any moment. Hope says, "Something good is going to happen to me today."

A positive attitude makes life simpler. It relieves pressure and puts a smile on your face. It is the attitude God wants us to have so He can work His will in our life. If we are going to walk with God, we must agree with Him. After all, He knows the thoughts and plans He has for us, thoughts of welfare and peace, to give us hope in our final outcome (see Jeremiah 29:11).

95

Resist the Devil

"The meanest thing in the world is the devil."

—Henry Ward Beecher

So be subject to God. Resist the devil [stand firm against him], and he will flee from you.

—*James 4:7*

God's Word teaches us that if we submit ourselves to God and resist the devil, he will flee (see James 4:7). If we don't resist the devil's lies and temptations, he will eventually rule over us in every area. He is an aggressive enemy and we must not be passive about resisting him.

The devil wants our lives to be miserable and complicated. He wants to steal our joy, our peace, and every good thing Jesus died to give us. Decide today that you will exercise your rights as a child of God and enjoy the life He wants you to have. We often think if something is God's will for us, it will just automatically happen, but that is not true. We need to exercise our faith, which includes resisting the devil.

If you heard someone breaking into your home in the middle of the night, would you just lie in bed and assume God would take care of it? No, of course you wouldn't. You would jump out of bed, get something to use for protection, pray, and try to call for help. If you needed to, you would aggressively protect yourself and your family from the intruder. Why don't we behave the same way when the devil tries to break into our lives and steal God's good plan?

It is time to be more aggressive. If we stay *on* the attack we won't spend so much time *under* attack. Remember that God in you is greater than any enemy you have. The simple thing to do is resist the devil at his onset. The longer you wait, the more of a foothold he will gain.

96

Stay Spiritually Strong

"Sometimes the miracle of moving mountains is God granting you the strength to keep shoveling."

—SHANE LITTLEFIELD

The strong spirit of a man sustains him in bodily pain or *trouble.*

—*Proverbs 18:14*

Don't wait until you are in the middle of a terrible ordeal and then try to quickly get strong in spirit. It doesn't work that way. You must build up your reserves over time by spending the necessary time with God regularly, praying and studying His Word. It's foolish to wait until you need to pick up something heavy and then quickly try to build some muscle. You would never start working out at the gym one day and expect to lift three times your weight the next. We know we must build up muscle to pick up heavy things, and we should also know we must build spiritual strength to endure the trials of life without weakening.

I have discovered if I stay spiritually strong, many things no longer bother me, and in some cases, these were things that once upset me for days at a time. They were able to upset me because I wasn't strong enough in God to resist them properly or to even look at them in a right way. Our mind-set toward life's challenges has a lot to do with how we handle them and how they affect us emotionally. A man in the Bible named Joseph was sold into slavery by his own brothers, but he said that what the enemy meant for his harm, God intended for his good (see Genesis 50:20). He had a right attitude because he had a great relationship with God. He stayed spiritually strong at all times and experienced one victory after another.

Always being under condemnation, having a burden, or experiencing loss of peace or joy is very complicated and requires all our attention. It may seem like hard work to stay spiritually strong, but it is actually much simpler than always feeling overwhelmed by what is going on in life. Be strong in the Lord and in the power of His might (see Ephesians 6:10).

97

Be Faithful

"He who is faithful over a few things is a lord of cities. It does not matter whether you preach in Westminster Abbey, or teach a ragged class, so you be faithful. The faithfulness is all."

—George MacDonald

Many a man proclaims his own loving-kindness and *goodness, but a faithful man who can find?*

—*Proverbs 20:6*

Being faithful and seeing things through to completion is something very few people seem to know how to do. One may think giving up on something is easier, but the truth is, not living up to commitments can really complicate life. Unfaithful people end up with a lot of unfinished projects and a lifetime of making constant changes in job, church, relationships, and other important decisions. In reality, all these changes end up being more difficult than if people were faithful to begin with and finished what they started.

Even when it comes to marriage, many people give up when the going is rough; they get a divorce and soon they marry someone else and the cycle starts all over again. I always tell people to remember that even if the grass is greener on the other side, it will still need to be mowed. The fact is, any relationship worth having will have some imperfections and need some work. If we cannot work through conflict, we will never have good relationships.

If Dave had given up on me in the early years of our marriage, I might not be teaching God's Word all over the world today. Many people are what I call "diamonds in the rough." They have tremendous capability, and all they need is for someone to stick with them while they are shaped and polished. God is faithful and we need to be the same way. I encourage you to pray long and hard before you give up on anything. There may be a few times in life when quitting something is the only option, but quite often, giving up is the devil's trick to keep us frustrated and miserable. Stay faithful to what you've promised to do and believe that God will reward you for it.

98 Check Your Outlook

"Positive anything is better than negative nothing."
—Elbert Hubbard

My trust and *assured reliance* and *confident hope shall be fixed in Him.*

—Hebrews 2:13

What is your outlook on life? With what mind-set do you approach life? I want to remind you of something I said earlier in this book—our problem isn't life itself; it is our approach to living that causes us the most difficulty. Two people can have the same problem and one will be happy while the other is depressed and miserable. This tells me what's wrong isn't the problem itself; it's the way the problem is viewed—the approach—that's the difference.

Our approach to life is our own decision, and nobody can make us miserable if we decide we are going to be happy. If someone we know makes a bad choice, that does not mean we have to be miserable. Perhaps I have done my best in a situation, but a friend is still angry and dissatisfied. Does their bad attitude mean I now have to lose my joy? No, of course not! But I will have to *decide* not to let them steal my joy or they will. They decide how they will approach life, and I must also. They may decide to believe the worst, but I can still decide to believe the best. It does not take a genius to know which one of us is going to be happy and enjoy life.

Let me ask again—what is your outlook on life? Are you positive, always believing the best, and ready to show mercy and forgiveness to those who hurt you? Or are you depressed, discouraged, and discontent because everything didn't go the way you hoped? Pick your battles wisely and you will enjoy a life of simplicity. It is easier to have a positive outlook than it is to have a negative one.

99

With Humility Comes
Peace and Power

"If thou desire the love of God and man, be humble, for the proud heart, as it loves none but itself, is beloved of none but itself. Humility enforces where neither virtue, nor strength, nor reason can prevail."

—FRANCIS QUARLES

And the servant of the Lord must not be quarrelsome (fighting and contending). Instead, he must be kindly to everyone and mild-tempered [preserving the bond of peace]; he must be a skilled and suitable teacher, patient and forbearing and willing to suffer wrong.

—*2 Timothy 2:24*

Animosity is a wedge between individuals that opens a door for the devil to bring destruction. It is a negative emotion which complicates our lives and hurts our hearts and the hearts of others.

One of the ways to avoid animosity is to stay away from trifling, ill-informed controversies. When a person feels the need to always tell everyone what they think they know, they prove they really don't know anything at all. If they did, they would know they need to listen more than they talk. The Bible says contention only comes by pride. That means people cannot fight and argue unless pride is present.

Humility is the doorway to a simple, yet powerful life, lived joyfully. Humble yourself under God's mighty hand that He may exalt you in due time (see 1 Peter 5:6). Put on the same attitude and humble mind that Christ had (see Philippians 2:5). Humility values peace even more than trying to prove one is right. Humility is the highest virtue and a trait that must be sought ardently. It is also an open door to promotion and exaltation from God. A servant of God who avoids strife by being humble is someone who will enjoy a life of peace and power.

100 Let Discipline Be Your Friend

"The secret of discipline is motivation. When a man is sufficiently motivated, discipline will take care of itself."

—ALEXANDER PATTERSON

For God did not give us a spirit of timidity (of cowardice, of craven and cringing and fawning fear), but [He has given us a spirit] of power and of love and of calm and well-balanced mind and discipline and self-control.

—2 Timothy 1:7

The word *discipline* usually causes people to groan, but it actually should be seen as a good friend that helps us get what we want in life. Discipline helps us do what we know we should do, but probably will not do without help. Discipline helps us! You may be thinking, *Yes, but it sure hurts.* That is true, but it also brings order, good fruit, and eventually freedom.

One thing that hurts worse than learning discipline is a life that is a never-ending complicated mess. The pain of change is always better than the agony of never changing. Ask yourself if you would rather feel bad and be weak all your life, or instead, discipline yourself to exercise and enjoy feeling healthy and strong? Would you like to continue eating junk food and have bad health, or discipline yourself for changing to a healthier lifestyle and enjoy good health and long life? Would you like to be out of debt and be able to pay cash for what you need? Then you must discipline yourself to live within your means. Would you like your home to be neat, clean, and in order? If so, you must discipline yourself to keep it that way. It won't happen by any other means.

JOYCE MEYER is one of the world's leading practical Bible teachers. A #1 *New York Times* bestselling author, she has written more than seventy inspirational books, including *The Confident Woman; Look Great, Feel Great,* the entire Battlefield of the Mind family of books, and many others. She has also released thousands of audio teachings as well as a complete video library. Joyce's *Enjoying Everyday Life®* radio and television programs and broadcast around the world, and she travels extensively conducting conferences. Joyce and her husband, Dave, are the parents of four grown children and make their home in St. Louis, Missouri.

To contact the author in the United States:
Joyce Meyer Ministries
P.O. Box 655
Fenton, Missouri 63026
(636) 349-0303
www.joycemeyer.org

*Please include your testimony or help received
from this book when you write.
Your prayer requests are welcome.*

To contact the author in Canada:
Joyce Meyer Ministries-Canada, Inc.
Lambeth Box 1300
London, ON N6P IT5
(636) 349-0303

To contact the author in Australia:
Joyce Meyer Ministries-Australia
Locked Bag 77
Mansfield Delivery Centre
Queensland 4122
(07) 3349 1200

To contact the author in England:
Joyce Meyer Ministries
P.O. Box 1549
Windsor
SL4 1GT
Great Britain
+44 (0) 1753-831102

OTHER BOOKS BY JOYCE MEYER

The Power of Simple Prayer

The Everyday Life Bible

The Confident Woman

Look Great, Feel Great

Battlefield of the Mind*

Battlefield of the Mind Devotional

Battlefield of the Mind for Teens

Battlefield of the Mind for Kids

Approval Addiction

Ending Your Day Right

21 Ways to Finding Peace

The Secret Power of Speaking God's Word

Seven Things That Steal Your Joy

Starting Your Day Right

Beauty for Ashes (revised edition)

How to Hear from God*

Knowing God Intimately

The Power of Forgiveness

The Power of Determination

Joyce Meyer Spanish Titles

Las Siete Cosas Que Te Roban el Gozo
(Seven Things That Steal Your Joy)

Empezando Tu Dia Bien
(Starting Your Day Right)

*Study Guide available for this titles.

Books by Dave Meyer

Life Lines

CPSIA information can be obtained at www.ICGtesting.com
Printed in the USA
LVOW120502211011

251489LV00003B/105/P